# Correctional Health Care: Prison Health Care, Suicide Prevention: Lesson Plan and Participant's Manual

National Institute of Corrections:
U.S. Department of Justice

The BiblioGov Project is an effort to expand awareness of the public documents and records of the U.S. Government via print publications. In broadening the public understanding of government and its work, an enlightened democracy can grow and prosper. Ranging from historic Congressional Bills to the most recent Budget of the United States Government, the BiblioGov Project spans a wealth of government information. These works are now made available through an environmentally friendly, print-on-demand basis, using only what is necessary to meet the required demands of an interested public. We invite you to learn of the records of the U.S. Government, heightening the knowledge and debate that can lead from such publications.

Included are the following Collections:

Budget of The United States Government
Presidential Documents
United States Code
Education Reports from ERIC
GAO Reports
History of Bills
House Rules and Manual
Public and Private Laws

Code of Federal Regulations
Congressional Documents
Economic Indicators
Federal Register
Government Manuals
House Journal
Privacy act Issuances
Statutes at Large

# U.S. Department of Justice
# National Institute of Corrections

**Correctional Health Care: Suicide Prevention**

01-P603

**U. S. Department of Justice**

National Institute of Corrections

1960 Industrial Circle
Longmont, Colorado 80501

June 25, 2001

Dear Participant:

Welcome to the National Institute of Corrections Prison Division's training program, **Correctional Health Care: Suicide Prevention.** *This program will deal with many of the issues concerning suicide prevention programming that correctional systems are facing and will examine issues such as: detection, risk factors medical and mental health care, the management of these offenders; and more.*

This will be an active training program. To assist you in this learning experience, we urge you to interact with the faculty and fellow participants and share your expertise and management techniques. *As always, finding out what the other states are doing is a major benefit of any NIC program* it is frequently our experience that participants learn as much from one another, both in and out of the classroom, as they do from the rest of the program.

We are pleased to have your participation and hope that this is a valuable learning experience for you.

Sincerely,

Susan M. Hunter, Chief
NIC Prisons Division

Robert M. Brown, Jr., Chief
NIC Academy

# NATIONAL INSTITUTE OF CORRECTIONS

The National Institute of Corrections is a Federal agency established to assist correctional agencies at the Federal, state, and local levels.

## History and Mission

In September 1971, a major riot at New York's Attica prison focused national attention on corrections and the practice of imprisonment in the United States. In response to the public fervor incited by the handling of the riot by correctional administrators and elected officials, and recognizing the inadequacy of correctional personnel and programs at the state and local levels throughout the county, Attorney General John A. Mitchell convened the first National Conference on Corrections in Williamsburg, Virginia, in December of that year.

> *The National Institute of Corrections was established in 1974 following the riot at Attica and a recognition that agencies needed assistance.*

Chief Justice Warren Burger, in his keynote address before the 450 distinguished experts at the conference, recommended the establishment of a national training academy for corrections, a proposal that gave birth to the National Institute of Corrections (NIC). The Chief Justice, cognizant of the deficiencies in corrections and the lack of coordination and leadership, enunciated the vision of a national training academy that would:

- Encourage the development of a body of correctional knowledge, coordinate research, conduct executive training programs, and formulate policy recommendations;

- Provide professional training for correctional employees ranging from newly recruited personnel to top management;

- Provide a forum and exchange for the discussion and evaluation of advanced ideas in corrections; and

- Bring about the long-neglected professionalism of the field.

> *NIC conducts research, provides training, administers technical assistance, develops model policies, and acts as a clearinghouse.*

The National Institute of Corrections was started in 1974 in response to this recommendation. The Institute's founding legislation, Public Law 93-415, mandates that it provide training, technical assistance, clearinghouse services, research and policy/program formulation and development to improve federal, state, and local corrections. The institute was first funded in 1977, as a line item in the Federal

# NIC Overview

training activities and functions as a national training center for state and local correctional administrators, managers, and staff trainers. (See the overview of the Academy on the next pages.)

> *Information Center*
> *The Information Center is located in Longmont, CO and serves as a national clearinghouse on correctional topics. It can be reached at 800-877-1461.*

## Information Center

The NIC Information Center, also located in Longmont, is a contract operation that responds to the information needs of practitioners from all areas of corrections. It serves as the base for information and materials collection and dissemination for the Institute and as a national clearinghouse on correctional topics for federal, state, and local practitioners. The Information Center is available to serve correctional practitioners when they have an issue they are addressing. The services are free of charge.

## Academy

The Academy, a division of the National Institute of Corrections (NIC), began operation in Boulder, Colorado, on October 1, 1981, and provides training for state and local correctional practitioners. By developing and delivering training for prison, jail, and community corrections practitioners, the Academy serves as a catalyst for interaction among correctional agencies, other components of the criminal justice system, public policy makers (e.g., county commissioners, state legislators), and concerned public and private organizations.

> *Mission of the Academy*
> *Training today's correctional leaders to meet tomorrow's challenges.*

The mission of the Academy is to serve as a catalyst through training, technical assistance, and related services to enhance the leadership, professionalism, and effectiveness of correctional personnel in operating safe, efficient, humane and constitutional systems.

The Academy believes in, "Training today's correctional leaders to meet tomorrow's challenges." Through training, the Academy promotes constructive organizational change and full use of resources to maximize correctional agencies' abilities to operate in a fair, safe, efficient, humane, and constitutional manner. The Academy works closely with the other NIC Divisions and with the NIC Information Center.

All of the services of the Academy are provided free of charge to eligible constituents in state and local correctional agencies. The Academy also provides services on a limited basis, through interagency agreements and paid participation, to other Federal agencies (such as the Federal Bureau of Prisons) and to correctional agencies in other nations.

### Personnel

The chief of the Academy, along with the administrative assistant and budget analyst

> *Training Services*
> *Training services include training programs, workshops, video and audio-conferences, training materials, and DACUM profiles.*

Training Programs - The majority of the Academy budget is dedicated to training programs for correctional administrators, trainer development, and for special issues such as substance abuse programming. Programs are held either in Longmont, Colorado or on site, in partnership with state or local corrections agencies. Most training programs are four and a half days long and provide management training to executives such as wardens and associate wardens in prisons, sheriffs, jail administrators and top-level probation and parole agency administrators. Personnel of specialized areas (such as medical services) are also trained, sometimes in teams to have the greatest impact on their agencies. Trainers are trained in specialties such as needs assessment and evaluation, in addition to basic and advanced train-the-trainer training.

The Academy contracts with experts and practitioners nationally to develop and deliver the programs. Most expenses are paid for program participants, including travel, per diem, and materials. Applicants are screened carefully to meet the target audience specifications. They must have the signed endorsement of their agencies' top administrators to participate in training programs and are expected to train others as well as implement their action plans (typically required in programs) upon their return.

Workshops - The Academy also supports half-day to day-long workshops in conjunction with national level professional conferences, such as the annual meeting of the American Correctional Association. These conference workshops provide condensed versions of some of the most requested training programs, such as an overview of the substance abuse training, as well as opportunities to review new curriculum packages.

Videoconferences/Audioconferences - As the costs of travel and other expenses associated with face-to-face training escalate, the Academy is communicating and providing training through electronic technologies. One alternative is telephone meetings or audioconferencing, which is inexpensive and effective. The Academy uses audioconferences for: 1 to 2 hour meetings with consultants to plan programs or curriculum packages; meeting with Regional Field Coordinators; and follow-up sessions with training program participants to determine how successfully they implemented their action plans or used the skills learned in the training.

The second technology, video-conferencing, with one-way video and two-way audio, provides updates on current topics. The two-hour live interactive videoconferences provides training to thousands nationally and internationally (Canada) on topics such as "Managing Tuberculosis in the Corrections Environment" and "The Impact of the Americans with Disabilities Act on Corrections".

Training Materials - The Academy develops curriculum packages, such as Working with Female Offenders, that include lesson plans, participant materials, and training aids.

# Central Region
## Lillie Hopkins - NIC Coordinator
800-995-6429 extension 124

Ms. Sue Bradshaw
Employee Development Manager
FCI, P.O. Box 1731
1000 University Drive SW
Waseca, MN, 56093-0741
507-835-8972; e-mail:sbradshaw@bop.gov
C-Year(s) Served: 1999, 2000, 2001, 3rd Year; BOP

Mr. Robert L. Conrad, Training Officer
Ohio Department of Rehabilitation and Correction
Ross Correctional Institution, 16149 State Route 104
Chillicothe, OH, 54601
740-774-7050 x2313, Fax: 740-774-7068;
C-Year(s) Served: 2001, 1st Year; Prisons

Sgt. Brian Fink, Training Supervisor
Will County Sheriff's Department
95 South Chicago Street
Joliet, IL, 60431
815-740-5575, Fax: 815-740-5565;
e-mail: bfink@willcosheriff.org
C-Year(s) Served: 2001, 1st Year; Jail

Ms. Michele C. Foley
Director of Staff Development and Training
Department of Juvenile Justice
1025 Capital Center Drive
Frankfort, KY, 40601-2638
502-573-2738 x292; e-mail: mcfoley@mail.state.ky.us
C-Year(s) Served: 1999, 2000, 2001, 3rd Year; Juvenile

Mr. Dwight L. Graves
Supervisor of Program Development
Indiana Department of Corrections
320 West Washington Street, IGC-South E334
Indianapolis, IN, 46204
317-233-5235; Fax: 317-233-5728;
e-mail: Dgraves@COA.DOC.STATE.IN.US
C-Year(s) Served: 1999, 2000, 2001, 3rd Year; Community Corrections

Ms. Marlene S. Koopman
Training Coordinator
Iowa State Prison
PO Box 316
Ft. Madison, IA 52627
319-372-5432 x285; Fax: 319-372-9087;
e-mail: marlene.koopman@doc1.State.IA. US
C-Year(s) Served: 2000, 2001 2nd Year; Prison

Mr. Larry D. Mitchell
Employee Development Manager
Federal Medical Center
3301 Leestown Road
Lexington, KY, 40511
859-255-6812 x235; Fax: 859-253-8822;
e-mail: lmitchell@bop.gov
C-Year(s) Served: 1999, 2000, 2001, 3rd Year; BOP

Mr. Jay Nelson (Alumni Coordinator)
Correctional Treatment Manager
Mt. Pleasant Correctional Facility
1200 East Washington
Mt. Pleasant, IA 52659
319-385-9511 x2332; Fax: 319-385-8511;
e-mail: jay.nelson@DOC1.state.ia.us

Mr. Tim Tausend, Senior Personnel Officer
North Dakota Youth Correctional Center
701 16th Avenue SW
Mandan, ND, 58554
701-667-1465; Fax: 701-667-1414;
e-mail: tausend@state.nd.us
C-Year(s) Served: 1999, 2000, 2001, 3rd Year; Juvenile

Mr. Keith Williams
Corrections Training Officer
Missouri Department of Corrections, Eastern Region Tra Academy
PO Box 365
Park Hills, MO, 63601
314-426-2498; Fax: 314-426-4526 (primary)
573-431-2283; Fax: 573-518-0925 (secondary)
e-mail: kwilliams@mail.doc.state.mo.us
C-Year(s) Served: 2001, 1st Year; Community Correctio

Updated March 7, 2001

# SouthernRegion
## Leslie LeMaster - NIC Coordinator
800-995-6429 extension 121

Ms. Mary Gillette
Employee Development Manager
FMC Carswell
PO Box 27066
J Street Building 3000
Fort Worth, TX, 76127
817-782-4390; Fax: 817-782-4394;
e-mail: magillette@bop.gov
S-Year(s) Served: 1st Year; BOP

Mr. Jules T. Franklin
Director of Staff Development
Texas Youth Commission
8004 Cameron Road, Suite C
Austin, TX, 78754
512-340-2740; Fax: 512-340-2702;
e-mail: jules.franklin@tyc.state.tx.us
S-Year(s) Served: 1999, 2000, 2001, 3rd Year; Juvenile

Ms. Melissa Ann Fricker, Training Coordinator
South Carolina Depart. of Probation, Parole, and Pardon Services
PO Box 50666
Columbia, SC, 29250
808-734-9234; Fax: 803-734-9190;
e-mail: MFricker@PPP.state.sc.us
S-Year(s) Served: 2001 1st Year; Community Corrections

Ms. Karen M. Jett
Senior Staff Development/Training Coordinator
Georgia Department of Corrections
1000 Indian Springs Drive
Forsyth, GA, 31029
912-993-4575; Fax: 912-993-4454;
e-mail: jettk00@dcor.state.ga.us
S-Year(s) Served: 2001 1st Year; Prisons

Mr. Daniel W. Lilly, Jr.
Director, Office of Staff Development and Training
North Carolina Department of Correction
2211 Schieffelin Road
Apex, NC, 27502
919-367-7102; Fax: 919-367-7180;
e-mail: ldw01@doc.state.nc.us
S-Year(s) Served: 2001, 1st Year; Prisons

Mr. Bill O'Connell
Senior Management Analyst II
Florida Department of Juvenile Justice
5310 Clay Drive
Lakeland, FL, 33813
863-534-0231; Fax: 863-534-0239;
e-mail: Bill.O'Connell@djj.state.fl.us
S-Year(s) Served: 1999, 2000, 2001, 3rd Year; Juvenile

Mr. John D. Ostrander
Training Director
Dougherty County Sheriff's Office
P.O. Box 549
Albany, GA, 31702
912-430-6514; Fax: 912-430-6562;
e-mail: johnostrander@netscape.net
S-Year(s) Served: 1999, 2000, 2001, 3rd Year; Jails

Ms. Pam Perrin
Employee Development Manager
Federal Correctional Institution
100 Prison Road
Estill, SC, 29918
803-625-4607 x4656; Fax: 803-625-5614;
e-mail: pperrin@bop.gov
S-Year(s) Served: 2000, 2001 2nd Year; BOP

Mr. Michael E. Waters
Director of Training
Alabama Department of Corrections
351 Avenue C
Selma, AL, 36701
334-872-6228; Fax: 334-874-6046;
e-mail: mwaters@doc.state.al.us
S-Year(s) Served: 2000, 2001 2nd Year; Prison

Mr. Dennis White
Major/Academy Director
Jefferson County Sheriff's Department
5030 Hwy 69 South
Beaumont, TX, 77705
409-726-2521; Fax: 409-726-2511
S-Year(s) Served: 2001, 3rd Year; Jails

Updated March 7, 2001

# NIC Corrections Exchange:
## A Listserv for People Serious About Corrections

The NIC Corrections Exchange is a communication opportunity for corrections professionals, launched by NIC in 1998. It provides a public, online forum for discussing corrections issues and practices and for exchanging views and information. The Exchange also facilitates communication between the National Institute of Corrections and field practitioners, policy makers, researchers, and others concerned with corrections.

To Join--
- Send email to correx-request@www.nicic.org with the word "subscribe" in your message.
- Or, visit the NIC web site at http://www.nicic.org/lists.htm and click on "NIC open lists" and "NIC Corrections Exchange." Scroll down the entry page to the "join" boxes.

The system will ask you to confirm your email address and will send you user guidelines.

**NIC Information Center Web Site--http://www.nicic.org**
- Full-text, downloadable NIC publications
- Searchable database of NIC reports and publications
- NIC "What's New" updates
- NetConnections to web links relevant to corrections . . . and more!

**NIC Information Center**
1860 Industrial Circle, Suite A
Longmont, CO 80501
(800) 877-1461 or (303) 682-0213 -- fax (303) 682-0558
asknicic@nicic.org
http://www.nicic.org

# New Communication Technologies at NIC Information Center

Corrections practitioners, policy makers, and researchers now have two new ways to access NIC information and materials.

**NIC Information Center Web Site--http://www.nicic.org**

- Immediate access to downloadable, full-text NIC publications
- A searchable database of more than 1,200 publications developed by NIC or with NIC funding
- A What's New section, with NIC program and publication announcements
- NetConnections, with Internet links relevant to corrections
- Email links for ordering materials or requesting personal research assistance
- NIC's public listserv, the NIC Corrections Exchange

**Fax on Demand:**

Call into a menu system at **(303) 678-9049** and select items to be faxed directly to you. Selections are identified by an 8-digit number.

The system provides prominent, shorter publications and the NIC Service Plan. Users can request a list of titles currently on the system, or can view the current list from the Information Center web site at **http://www.nicic.org/faxtitles.htm.**

## NIC Information Center
1860 Industrial Circle, Suite A
Longmont, CO 80501
(800) 877-1461 or (303) 682-0213 -- fax (303) 682-0558
asknicic@nicic.org
http://www.nicic.org

NATIONAL INSTITUTE OF CORRECTIONS
NATIONAL INSTITUTE OF CORRECTIONS PRISONS

**Prison Health Care: Suicide Prevention**
01-P603

Raintree Plaza Hotel & Conference Center
Longmont, Colorado

Silverthorne Room
June 25 - 29, 2001

## *Training Program Goal*

*This training will examine issues around suicide and provide current information and resources regarding suicide prevention programs for offenders incarcerated in adult institutions.*

### *Training Program Objectives*

*At the conclusion of this training participants will be able to:*

- *Identify programmatic guidelines for suicidal inmates*
- *Identify common health-based risk factors for suicide*
- *Discuss various methods of suicide prevention*
- *Analyze methods your department can employ to ensure you have effective suicide prevention program policies and procedures.*

## NATIONAL INSTITUTE OF CORRECTIONS
## NATIONAL INSTITUTE OF CORRECTIONS PRISONS

### Prison Health Care: Suicide Prevention
01-P603

| | |
|---|---|
| **Raintree Plaza Hotel & Conference Center** | **Silverthorne Room** |
| **Longmont, Colorado** | **June 25 - 29, 2001** |

### June 25, 2001

6:00 - 7:30 pm  Dinner

7:30 - 9:00 pm  Introductions and Overview                               Madeline Ortiz

        Participant Introductions
        Staff Introductions
        Purpose of Training Program
        NIC History

### June 26, 2001

8:00 - 8:30  NIC Information Center                                      Pat Skoles

        Program Overview                                         Madeline Ortiz
            Agenda
            Objectives
            Housekeeping

8:30 - 10:00  Suicide Prevention:
            Importance of Issue to Prison
            Administrators and Clinicians                Lindsay Hayes

        Why is This Important
            Safety of Staff and Inmates (preservation of life)
            Reduce Disruptions in Operations
            Risk Management
            Reducing Liability
        What is Suicide and How Frequently Does it Occur
            Definitions (grid)
            Research and Statistics (risk factors)

**June 27, 2001** continued

| | | |
|---|---|---|
| 3:00-3:15 | BREAK | |
| 3:15- 4:45 | Aftermath of a Suicide<br>    Reporting<br>    Mortality Review<br>    Critical Incident Stress Debriefing<br>    Development of Corrective Actions | Lindsay Hayes |
| 4:45-5:00 | Wrap up | |

**June 28, 2001**

| | | |
|---|---|---|
| 8:00- 10:00 | Panel: Emerging Ideas | Teena Farmon,<br>Lindsay Hayes<br>Bonita Vesey<br>Fred Maue |
| 10:00 - 11:00 | Q & A, Evaluations, Certificates | |

**Bonita M. Veysey, Ph.D.** is presently Assistant Professor and Director of the Center for Justice and Mental Health Research at Rutgers University, School of Criminal Justice. She is currently involved in several projects through the Center. She is co-principal investigator on a five-year outcome study of comprehensive services for women with co-occurring disorders and histories of trauma; she is the Principal Investigator on an evaluation of an eleven county diversion program for justice-involved youth with co-occurring disorders in New York State; and she is a co-principal investigator on a detailed study of health and behavioral health care in New Jersey jails. Formerly, Dr. Veysey was employed as a Senior Research Associate at Policy Research Associates and has served as the Director of the Women's Program within the National GAINS Center for People with Co-Occurring Disorders in the Justice System. Dr. Veysey has conducted multi-site national research projects in the area of jail services and was the principal staff member on a CMHS report to Congress, "Double Jeopardy: Persons with Mental Illnesses in the Criminal Justice System." She has written several articles on specific needs of women with substance abuse and mental disorders in the criminal justice system and has consulted with correctional facilities regarding the need for services for female offenders and for persons with mental illnesses.

**Brief Biography
of
LINDSAY M. HAYES**

Lindsay M. Hayes is the Assistant Director of the National Center on Institutions and Alternatives, with an office in Mansfield, Massachusetts. Mr. Hayes is nationally recognized as an expert in the field of suicides within jails, prisons and juvenile facilities. As a consultant, he conducts training seminars and assesses suicide prevention practices in various state and local correctional systems throughout the country. Mr. Hayes has serves as an expert witness/consultant in suicide litigation cases.

Further, he has conducted the only three national studies of jail and prison suicide for the U.S. Justice Department, as well as co-authored a model training curriculum on jail suicide prevention. He is currently completing the first national study of juvenile suicide in confinement, as well as a model training curriculum on juvenile suicide prevention..

As a result of research, technical assistance, and expert witness/consultant work in the area of suicide prevention in correctional facilities, Mr. Hayes has reviewed and/or examined over 1,500 cases of suicide in jail, prison, and juvenile facilities throughout the country during the past 20 years.

Finally, Mr. Hayes serves as editor of the *Jail Suicide/Mental Health Update*, a quarterly newsletter that is funded by the U.S. Justice Department, and has authored over 50 publications in the area of suicide prevention within correctional facilities.

February 2001 (revised)

National Institute of Corrections
Prisons Division

# PRISON HEALTH CARE: SUICIDE PREVENTION
01-P603

June 25-28, 2001

presented by
**Lindsay M. Hayes**

## LESSON PLAN

# Suicide Prevention: Importance of Issue to Prison Administrators and Clinicians
(June 26, 2001, 8:30-10:00am)

# Introduction
## OVERCOMING OBSTACLES TO PREVENTION

Experience has shown that negative attitudes often impede meaningful prison suicide prevention efforts. Such attitudes form *obstacles to prevention*, and can be seen on both a local and universal basis. Simply stated, obstacles to prevention are empty excuses that inmate suicides can not be prevented. For example, **a local obstacle** might sound something like this:

- "We did everything we could to prevent this death, but he showed no signs of suicidal behavior;"

- "There's no way you can prevent suicides unless you have someone sitting watching the prisoner all the time, and no one can afford to be a baby sitter;"

- "We didn't consider him suicidal, he was simply being manipulative and I guess it just went too far;"

- "We aren't mind readers nor trained to be psychiatrists;"

- "If someone really wants to kill themselves, there's generally nothing you can do about it;"

- "Suicide prevention is a medical problem...it's a mental health problem...it's not our problem."

Then there are **universal obstacles** to prevention -- regressive attitudes that are far more dangerous because of their far-reaching ability to negatively influence correctional policy on a larger scale. We often find the roots of this attitude in the world of academia:

- o "Statistically speaking, suicide in custody is a rare phenomenon, and rare phenomena are notoriously difficult to forecast due to their low base rate. We cannot predict suicide because social scientists are not fully aware of the casual variables involving suicide;"

- o "Demographic profiles of custodial suicide victims are of little value for prediction because they often mirror the characteristics of typical jail or prison inmates;"

- o "Even those skilled mental health professionals, who have the time for extensive personal interaction with troubled individuals, either cannot forecast suicide or are unable to prevent patient suicide even if it had been somewhat anticipated;"

- o "Jail and prison suicides are extremely difficult to predict due to their spontaneous nature;" and

- o "To speak bluntly, custodial suicide may constitute less a readily solvable problem than a situation which, in view of our present knowledge and our financial limitations, may be expected to continue."

There are various ways to defuse these local and universal obstacles, the most appropriate of which is to demonstrate successful interventions.

For example, with over 5,000 inmates, the Orange County Jail System in Santa Ana, California, is the 12th largest jail system in the country, and 3rd largest in California. During the past 10 years, over 831,040 have been processed through the system and only 5 inmates have successfully committed suicide. The suicide rate in the Orange County Jail System (9.4 deaths per 100,000 inmates). Why? Because of the ATTITUDE.

**"WHEN YOU BEGIN TO USE EXCUSES TO JUSTIFY A BAD OUTCOME, WHETHER IT BE LOW STAFFING LEVELS, INADEQUATE FUNDING, PHYSICAL PLANT CONCERNS, ETC. -- ISSUES WE STRUGGLE WITH EACH DAY -- YOU LACK THE PHILOSOPHY...THAT EVEN ONE DEATH IS NOT ACCEPTABLE. IF YOU ARE GOING TO TOLERATE A FEW DEATHS IN YOUR CORRECTIONAL SYSTEM, THEN YOU'VE ALREADY LOST THE BATTLE."**

> Jail Commander
> Orange County (California)

# JAIL AND PRISON SUICIDE RESEARCH

## Jails

o There are over 400 jail suicides (excluding prisons) each year, and suicide is the leading cause of death in jails throughout the country

o The rate of suicide in county jails is estimated to be 107 deaths per 100,000 inmates or a rate that is approximately 9 times greater than in the community

o Most jail suicides occur within the first 24 hours of incarceration; most victims were isolated from both staff and inmates and not screened for potentially suicidal behavior at intake

## Prisons

o There are over 160 prison suicides each year, and suicide is the third leading cause of death in prisons, behind Natural Causes and AIDS

o The rate of suicide in prisons is estimated to be between 15 and 17 deaths per 100,000 inmates or a rate that is approximately 20-25 percent greater than in the community

o The majority of prison suicide victims had documented histories of mental illness and suicidal behavior; many victims were housed in administrative segregation at the time of their deaths

# TOTAL PRISON SUICIDES AND RATES BY STATE (1984-1993)

| State | Suicides | Total Inmate Population | Rate |
|---|---|---|---|
| Alabama | 17 | 122,117 | 13.9 |
| Alaska* | 20 | 22,921 | 87.3 |
| Arizona | 38 | 125,059 | 30.4 |
| Arkansas | 13 | 59,459 | 21.9 |
| California | 176 | 779,724 | 22.6 |
| Colorado | 17 | 54,005 | 31.5 |
| Connecticut* | 32 | 85,857 | 37.3 |
| Delaware* | 7 | 30,625 | 22.9 |
| District of Columbia* | 13 | 83,309 | 15.6 |
| Florida | 43 | 385,035 | 11.2 |
| Georgia | 34 | 205,828 | 16.5 |
| Hawaii* | 7 | 22,416 | 31.2 |
| Idaho | 7 | 16,763 | 41.8 |
| Illinois | 38 | 242,998 | 15.6 |
| Indiana | 20 | 117,613 | 17.0 |
| Iowa | 6 | 37,667 | 15.9 |
| Kansas | 12 | 53,604 | 22.4 |
| Kentucky | 14 | 66,357 | 21.1 |
| Louisiana | 28 | 128,667 | 21.8 |
| Maine | 9 | 13,325 | 67.5 |
| Maryland | 30 | 154,341 | 19.4 |
| Massachusetts | 26 | 79,177 | 32.8 |
| Michigan | 43 | 258,742 | 16.6 |
| Minnesota | 27 | 30,584 | 88.3 |
| Mississippi | 17 | 70,443 | 24.1 |
| Missouri | 25 | 129,297 | 19.3 |
| Montana | 10 | 12,076 | 82.8 |
| Nebraska | 10 | 22,024 | 45.4 |
| Nevada | 21 | 49,989 | 42.0 |
| New Hampshire | 3 | 11,612 | 25.8 |
| New Jersey | 26 | 150,391 | 17.3 |
| New Mexico | 2 | 28,134 | 7.1 |
| New York | 53 | 482,915 | 11.0 |
| North Carolina | 25 | 184,832 | 13.5 |
| North Dakota | 5 | 4,917 | 101.7 |
| Ohio | 49 | 286,364 | 17.1 |
| Oklahoma | 32 | 93,380 | 34.3 |
| Oregon | 13 | 51,497 | 25.2 |
| Pennsylvania | 49 | 189,297 | 25.9 |
| Rhode Island* | 12 | 20,410 | 58.8 |
| South Carolina | 21 | 130,515 | 16.1 |
| South Dakota | 6 | 12,078 | 49.7 |
| Tennessee | 23 | 83,624 | 27.5 |
| Texas | 89 | 451,677 | 19.7 |
| Utah | 13 | 21,834 | 59.5 |
| Vermont* | 3 | 7,468 | 40.2 |
| Virginia | 28 | 136,814 | 20.5 |
| Washington | 22 | 72,394 | 30.4 |
| West Virginia | 3 | 15,175 | 19.8 |
| Wisconsin | 10 | 66,509 | 15.0 |
| Wyoming | 6 | 8,821 | 68.0 |
| Federal Bur. of Prisons* | 86 | 528,541 | 16.3 |
| **Total** | **1,339** | **6,499,221** | **20.6** |

*Dual System of Both Pre-Trial and Sentenced Inmates

**SOURCE:** Hayes, Lindsay M. (1995). *Prison Suicide: An Overview and Guide to Prevention*. Washington, D.C.: National Institute of Corrections U.S. Department of Justice.

# TOTAL PRISON SUICIDES AND RATES
# (1984-1993)

| Year | Suicides | Total Inmates | Rate |
|---|---|---|---|
| 1984 | 121 | 446,212 | 27.1 |
| 1985 | 132 | 485,301 | 27.2 |
| 1986 | 126 | 522,780 | 24.1 |
| 1987 | 139 | 554,654 | 25.1 |
| 1988 | 139 | 598,239 | 23.2 |
| 1989 | 146 | 672,193 | 21.7 |
| 1990 | 118 | 730,486 | 16.2 |
| 1991 | 127 | 774,198 | 16.4 |
| 1992 | 133 | 825,322 | 16.1 |
| 1993 | 158 | 889,836 | 17.8 |
| TOTAL | 1,339 | 6,499,221 | 20.6 |

**SOURCE:** Hayes, Lindsay M. (1995). *Prison Suicide: An Overview and Guide to Prevention*. Washington, D.C.: National Institute of Corrections U.S. Department of Justice.

| | | | |
|---|---|---|---|
| 1995 | 169 | 992,333 | 17.0 |
| 1997 | 159 | 1,059,607 | 15.0 |

**SOURCE:** Bureau of Justice Statistics, U.S. Department of Justice, 1995 and 1997.

**HOUSING:** 6 (50%) in SEGREGATION (including 1 on death row

**SUICIDE PRECAUTIONS:** NONE

**MENTAL HEALTH CASELOAD:** 5 (42%)

**PREVIOUS SUICIDE ATTEMPT HISTORY:** 5 (42%)

**POSSIBLE PRECIPITATING FACTORS (IN 7 CASES):**

1) 1 year anniversary of close friend's death; depressed regarding proposed cut in college program

2) occurred shortly after parole board hearing in which he received a 4-year set off and inquiry regarding sexual offense history (correctional staff did intervene following hearing to assure to was okay with board's decision)

3) 3 days shy of 21st birthday (1); occurred on 30th birthday (1)

4) missed scheduled visit with psychiatrist 2 weeks earlier; feared transfer to Lucasville

5) perhaps feeling anxiety from accumulating drug debt

6) trouble in housing unit, fear of attack, previously raped in another facility

2) **TEXAS (1980-1985)**     N=38

   o 97% of suicides occurred in single cells

   o 45% of victims had prior history of suicidal behavior

   o 68% of victims had mental health histories

   o 58% of victims convicted of personal crimes

3) **NEW YORK (1986-1994)**     N=52

   o 23% of victims were serving life sentences

   o 64% of victims had sentences of 10 years or more

   o 48% of suicides occurred less than 12 months into confinement; additional 16% between 1-2 years

   o 80% of victims convicted of personal crimes (56% of population)

   o White inmates represented 42% of suicides (18% of population)

   o African American inmates represented 20% of suicides (50% of population)

   o Hispanic inmates represented 32% of suicides (31% of population)

## 4) Federal Bureau of Prisons (1988-1992)  N=43

- 53% of victims had mental health histories

- 42% of victims had prior history of suicidal behavior (including at least 1 attempt or gesture)

- 72% of suicides were by hanging

- 63% of victims were in segregation, administrative detention or psychiatric seclusion

- Pre-trial inmates and Mariel Cuban detainees accounted for 42% of suicides (10% of population)

- 28% of victims had sentences of 20 years or more (12% of population)

## Possible Precipitating Factors (via Clinical Review)

- New Legal Problems found in 28% of suicides

- Marital or Other Relationship Problems found in 23% of suicides

- Inmate-Related Conflicts found in 23% of suicides

# Suicide Prevention: Standards of Care and Liability
(June 26, 2001, 2:45-4:45pm)

# STANDARDS OF CARE

1) **National Commission on Correctional Health Care**

    *Standards for Health Services in Prisons* (1997)

    *Correctional Mental Health Care: Standards and Guidelines for Delivering Services* (1999)

    (contains "Guide to Developing and Revising Suicide Prevention Protocols")

2) **American Correctional Association**

    *Standards for Adult Correctional Institutions* (1990)

3) **American Psychiatric Association**

    *Psychiatric Services in Jails in Prisons* (2000)

    (contains suicide prevention standard identical to NCCHC standards)

# NCCHC Standard J-53: SUICIDE PREVENTION (1997)

Written policy and defined procedures require, and actual practice demonstrates, that the prison has a program for identifying and responding to suicidal inmates. The program components include training, identification, monitoring, referral, evaluation, housing, communication, intervention, notification, reporting, review, and critical incident debriefing.

**Discussion.** While inmates may become suicidal at any point during their stay, high-risk periods include the time immediately upon admission to the prison facility; following new legal problems (e.g., new charges/additional sentences, institutional proceedings, denial of parole); following the receipt of bad news regarding self or family (e.g., serious illness or the loss of a loved one); and after suffering some type of humiliation or rejection (e.g.., sexual assault). Inmates entering and/or unable to cope with administrative segregation or other specialized single-cell housing assignments are also at increased risk of suicide. In addition, inmates who are in the early stages of recovery from severe depression may be at risk as well.

Key components of a suicide prevention program include the following:

**1) Identification.** The receiving screening form should contain observation and interview items related to the inmate's potential suicide risk.

**2) Training.** All staff members who work with inmates should be trained to recognize verbal and behavioral cues that indicate potential suicide. The plan should include initial and subsequent training.

**3) Assessment.** This should be conducted by a qualified mental health professional, who designates the inmate's level of suicide risk.

**4) Monitoring.** The plan should specify the facility's procedures for monitoring an inmate who has been identified as potentially suicidal. Regular, documented supervision should be maintained.

**5) Housing.** A suicidal inmate should not be housed or left alone. An appropriate level of observation must be maintained. If a sufficiently large staff is not available that constant supervision can be provided when needed, the inmate should not be isolated. Rather, s/he should be housed with another resident or in a dormitory and checked every 10-15 minutes. An inmate assessed as being a high suicide risk always should be observed on a continuing, uninterrupted basis or transferred to an appropriate health care facility. The room should be as nearly suicide-proof as possible (i.e., without protrusions of any kind that would enable the inmate to hang him/herself).

**6) Referral.** The plan should specify the procedures for referring potentially suicidal inmates and attempted suicides to mental health care providers or facilities.

**7) Communication.** Procedures should exist for communication between health care and correctional personnel regarding the status of the inmate.

**8) Intervention.** The plan should address how to handle a suicide in progress, including appropriate first-aid measures.

**9) Notification.** Procedures should be in place for notifying jail administrators, outside authorities, and family members of potential, attempted, or completed suicides.

**10 Reporting.** Procedures for documenting the identification and monitoring of potential or attempted suicides should be detailed, as should procedures for reporting a completed suicide.

**11) Review.** The plan should specify the procedures for medical and administrative review if a suicide or a serious suicide attempt (as defined by the suicide plan) does occur.

**12) Critical incident debriefing.** Responding to and/or observing a suicide in progress can be extremely stressful for staff and inmates. The plan should specify the procedures for offering critical incident debriefing to all affected personnel and inmates.

# ACA Standard 3-4364
# Suicide Prevention and Intervention

There is a written suicide prevention and intervention program that is reviewed and approved by a qualified medical or mental health professional. All staff with responsibility for inmate supervision are trained in the implementation of the program.

*Comment.* The program should include specific procedures for intake screening, identification, and supervision of suicide-prone inmates.

# SUICIDE PREVENTION POLICY

All correctional facilities, regardless of size, should have a detailed written suicide prevention policy that addresses each of the following critical components:

## 1) TRAINING

*All* correctional, medical, and mental health staff should receive eight (8) hours of initial suicide prevention training, followed by two (2) hours of annual training. Training should include why jail environments are conducive to suicidal behavior, potential pre-disposing factors to suicide, high-risk suicide periods, warning signs and symptoms, and components of the facility's suicide prevention policy.

## 2) IDENTIFICATION/SCREENING

Intake screening for suicide risk must take place immediately upon confinement and prior to housing assignment. This process may be contained within the medical screening form or as a separate form, and must include inquiry regarding: past suicidal ideation and/or attempts; current ideation, threat, plan; prior mental health treatment/hospitalization; recent significant loss (job, relationship, death of family member/close friend, etc.); history of suicidal behavior by family member/close friend; suicide risk during prior contact/confinement with agency; and arresting/transporting officer(s) believes inmate is currently at risk. Process must include procedures for referral to mental health and/or medical personnel.

## 3) COMMUNICATION

Procedures that enhance communication at three levels: 1) between the arresting/transporting officer(s) and jail staff; 2) between and among jail staff (including medical and mental health personnel); and 3) between jail staff and the suicidal inmate.

## 4) HOUSING

Isolation should be avoided. Whenever possible, house in general population, mental health unit, or medical infirmary, located in close proximity to staff. Inmates should be housed in suicide-resistant, protrusion-free cells. Removal of an inmate's clothing (excluding belts and shoelaces), as well as use of physical restraints (e.g. handcuffs, straitjackets, leather straps, etc.) should be avoided whenever possible, and only utilized as a last resort for periods in which the inmate is physically engaging in self-destructive behavior. These decisions should be made in collaboration with medical and/or mental health staff.

## 5) LEVELS OF SUPERVISION

Two levels of supervision are generally recommended for suicidal inmates -- *close observation* and *constant observation*. *Close Observation* is reserved for the inmate who is not actively suicidal, but expresses suicidal ideation and/or has a recent prior history of self-destructive behavior. This inmate should be observed by staff at staggered intervals not to exceed every 15 minutes. *Constant Observation* is reserved for the inmate who is actively suicidal, either by threatening or engaging in the act of suicide. This inmate should be observed by a staff member on a continuous, uninterrupted basis. Other supervision aids, (e.g. closed circuit television, inmate companions/watchers, etc.) can be utilized as a supplement to, but never as a substitute for, these observation levels.

## 6) INTERVENTION

A facility's policy regarding intervention should be threefold: 1) all staff who come into contact with inmates should be trained in standard first aid and cardiopulmonary resuscitation (CPR); 2) any staff member who discovers an inmate attempting suicide should immediately respond, survey the scene to ensure the emergency is genuine, alert other staff to call for medical personnel, and begin standard first aid and/or CPR; and 3) staff should never presume that the inmate is dead; but rather initiate and continue appropriate life-saving measures until relieved by arriving medical personnel. In addition, all housing units should contain a first aid kit, pocket mask or mouth shield, Ambu bag, and rescue tool (to quickly cut through fibrous material).

## 7) REPORTING

In the event of a suicide attempt or suicide, all appropriate jail officials should be notified through the chain of command. Following the incident, the victim's family should be immediately notified, as well as appropriate outside authorities. All staff who came into contact with the victim prior to the incident should be required to submit a statement as to their full knowledge of the inmate and incident.

## 8) FOLLOW-UP/ADMINISTRATIVE REVIEW

Every completed suicide, as well as serious suicide attempt (i.e. requiring hospitalization), should be examined by an administrative review. If resources permit, clinical review through a psychological autopsy is also recommended. All staff involved in the incident should participate in each process, as well as offered critical incident stress debriefing. Ideally, the reviews should be coordinated by an outside agency to ensure impartiality. An administrative review, separate and apart from other formal investigations that may be required to determine the cause of death, should include: 1) critical review of the circumstances surrounding the incident; 2) critical review of jail procedures relevant to the incident; 3) synopsis of all relevant training received by involved staff; 4) pertinent medical and mental health services/reports involving the victim; and 5) recommendations, if any, for change in policy, training, physical plant, medical or mental health services, and operational procedures.

# STATE STANDARDS AND *PRISON* SUICIDE PREVENTION: A REPORT CARD

- 79% of prison systems had a suicide prevention policy (15% did not have a policy, but some protocols found in other directives)

- 6% of prison systems did not address the issue of suicide prevention at all

- 52% addressed the issue of **Staff Training**

- 75% addressed the issue of **Housing**

- 79% addressed the issue of **Supervision**, but the highest level of supervision varied considerably:

    - 34% listed constant watch

    - 44% listed 15-minute watch

    - 20% listed 5- to 10-minute watch

    - 2% listed 30-minute watch

- 23% addressed the issue of **Intervention**

- 27% addressed the issue of **Mortality Review**

**SOURCE:** Hayes, Lindsay M. (1995). *Prison Suicide: An Overview and Guide to Prevention*. Washington, D.C.: National Institute of Corrections U.S. Department of Justice.

# LIABILITY ISSUES IN PRISON SUICIDE

TWO ROADS TO THE COURTHOUSE: **TORT SUIT** AND **CIVIL RIGHTS CLAIM**.

**1. TORT SUIT:** This claim alleges only that the defendant was negligent in a way which caused, or failed to prevent, the suicide. A tort suit seeks only damages.

**1. CIVIL RIGHTS ACTION:** This claim, brought pursuant to 42 USC Section 1983, alleges that a person, acting under color of state law, violated or acted with "deliberate indifference" in causing a violation of the decedent's constitutional rights. A civil rights action can seek both compensatory and punitive damages, as well as injunctive relief.

## WHAT IS <u>DELIBERATE INDIFFERENCE</u>?

o   IT HAS BEEN DEFINED AS "<u>APATHY</u> OR <u>UNCONCERN</u>"

o   IT HAS BEEN DEFINED AS CONDUCT THAT IS BELOW <u>MALICIOUS</u> OR <u>SADISTIC</u> BUT HIGHER THAN <u>MALPRACTICE</u> OR <u>NEGLIGENCE</u>

o   MORE APPROPRIATELY, IT HAS BEEN DEFINED AS "<u>CRIMINAL RECKLESSNESS</u>" -- <u>A CONSCIOUS DISREGARD OF A HIGH RISK OF HARM</u>

o   IT HAS BEEN, HOWEVER, A VERY "JAIL-FRIENDLY" LEGAL STANDARD IN LITIGATION OF JAIL SUICIDES

IN *FARMER v. BRENNAN* [114 S.Ct. 1970 (1994)], THE U.S. SUPREME COURT HAS FURTHER REFINED "DELIBERATE INDIFFERENCE" BY USING THE <u>SUBJECTIVE</u> STANDARD ("ACTUAL KNOWLEDGE"), RATHER THAN THE <u>OBJECTIVE</u> STANDARD ("OUGHT TO HAVE KNOWN"):

> WE HOLD INSTEAD THAT A PRISON OFFICIAL CANNOT BE FOUND LIABLE UNDER THE EIGHTH AMENDMENT FOR DENYING AN INMATE HUMANE CONDITIONS OF CONFINEMENT UNLESS THE OFFICIAL KNOWS OF AND DISREGARDS AN EXCESSIVE RISK OF INMATE HEALTH AND SAFETY; <u>THE OFFICIAL MUST BE AWARE BOTH OF FACTS FROM WHICH THE INFERENCE CAN BE DRAWN THAT A SUBSTANTIAL RISK OF SERIOUS HARM EXISTS, AND HE MUST ALSO DRAW THE INFERENCE</u>...

> ...WE DOUBT THAT A SUBJECTIVE APPROACH WILL PRESENT PRISON OFFICIALS WITH ANY SERIOUS MOTIVATION TO TAKE REFUGE IN THE ZONE BETWEEN 'IGNORANCE OF OBVIOUS RISKS' AND THE 'ACTUAL KNOWLEDGE OF RISKS'...<u>A FACTFINDER MAY CONCLUDE THAT A PRISON OFFICIAL KNEW OF A SUBSTANTIAL RISK FROM THE VERY FACT THAT THE RISK WAS OBVIOUS</u>...

> ...FOR EXAMPLE, IF AN EIGHTH AMENDMENT PLAINTIFF PRESENTS EVIDENCE SHOWING THAT A SUBSTANTIAL RISK OF INMATE ATTACKS WAS '<u>LONGSTANDING, PERVASIVE, WELL-DOCUMENTED, OR EXPRESSLY NOTED

BY PRISON OFFICIALS IN THE PAST, AND THE CIRCUMSTANCES SUGGEST THAT THE DEFENDANT-OFFICIAL BEING SUED HAS BEEN EXPOSED TO INFORMATION CONCERNING THE RISK AND THUS 'MUST HAVE KNOWN' ABOUT IT, THEN SUCH EVIDENCE COULD BE SUFFICIENT TO PERMIT A TRIER OF FACT TO FIND THAT THE DEFENDANT-OFFICIAL HAD ACTUAL KNOWLEDGE OF THE RISK...

...THE QUESTION UNDER THE EIGHTH AMENDMENT IS WHETHER PRISON OFFICIALS, ACTING WITH DELIBERATE INDIFFERENCE, EXPOSED A PRISONER TO A SUFFICIENTLY SUBSTANTIAL 'RISK OF SERIOUS DAMAGE TO HIS FUTURE HEALTH'...AND IT DOES NOT MATTER WHETHER THE RISK COMES FROM A SINGLE SOURCE OR MULTIPLE SOURCES, ANY MORE THAN IT MATTERS WHETHER A PRISONER FACES EXCESSIVE RISK OF ATTACK FOR REASONS PERSONAL TO HIM OR BECAUSE ALL PRISONERS IN HIS SITUATION FACE SUCH A RISK...

...PRISON OFFICIALS WHO ACTUALLY KNEW OF A SUBSTANTIAL RISK TO INMATE HEATH OR SAFETY MAY BE FOUND FREE FROM LIABILITY IF THEY RESPONDED REASONABLY TO THE RISK EVEN IF THE HARM ULTIMATELY WAS NOT AVERTED...

IN INTERPRETING ***FARMER***, A PLAINTIFF ATTORNEY IN PRISON SUICIDE CASES WILL TRY DIFFERENT STRATEGIES, INCLUDING:

1) **INDIVIDUAL v. GENERALIZED RISK**: USING THE ***FARMER*** LANGUAGE OF IT DOES NOT "MATTER WHETHER THE PRISONER FACES AN EXCESSIVE RISK OF ATTACK FOR REASONS PERSONAL TO HIM OR BECAUSE <u>ALL PRISONERS IN HIS SITUATION FACE SUCH A RISK</u>," THEY WILL ARGUE THAT CERTAIN INMATES BELONG TO IDENTIFIABLE GROUPS KNOWN TO BE VULNERABLE AND THIS GENERALIZABLE RISK RENDERS JAILERS DELIBERATELY INDIFFERENT WHEN THEY FAIL TO TAKE REASONABLE PREVENTIVE MEASURES.

2) **REPEATED EXAMPLES OF NEGLIGENCE MIGHT RISE TO DELIBERATE INDIFFERENCE**: A PLAINTIFF ATTORNEY MIGHT ARGUE THAT DELIBERATE INDIFFERENCE MIGHT OCCUR FOLLOWING REPEATED EXAMPLES OF NEGLIGENCE WHICH DISCLOSE A PATTERN OF CONDUCT BY PRISON STAFF. WHILE A SINGLE ACT VIEWED IN ISOLATION MAY APPEAR TO BE THE PRODUCT OF NEGLIGENCE, REPEATED EXAMPLES OF SUCH TREATMENT BESPEAK A DELIBERATE INDIFFERENCE BY OFFICIALS OR STAFF.

# JAIL AND PRISON SUICIDE LITIGATION: CASE LAW REVIEW

1) *Tittle v. Jefferson County Commission* [10 F. 3rd 1535 (11th Cir. 1994)]

2) *Natriello v. Flynn* [837 F. Supp. 17 (D. Mass. 1993) and 36 ATLA L. Rep. 368 (Dec. 1993)]

3) *Heflin v. Stewart County* [958 F.2d 709 (6th Cir. 1992)]

4) *Simmons v. City of Philadelphia* [947 F.2d 1042 (3rd Cir. 1991)]

5) *Cunningham v. Tkadletz* [97 C 1109, Federal District Court for the Northern District of Illinois, 1998]

6) *Jacobs v. West Feliciana Sheriff's Department* [WL 1289478, 5th Cir., 2000]

# JAIL AND PRISON SUICIDE LITIGATION: CASE LAW REVIEW

*Listed below are case summaries of significant jail and prison suicide litigation compiled by Lindsay M. Hayes. This listing is not intended to be all inclusive. Revised May 2001.*

1) *Tittle v. Jefferson County Commission* [10 F. 3rd 1535 (11th Cir. 1994)]. Between October 1987 and December 1989, 57 suicide attempts occurred in the county jail, including four successful suicides within the 12-month period of September 1988 and 1989. The majority of these incidents involved hangings from various window bars or pipes in the facility. Each pipe, measuring six inches in diameter and filled with concrete, was located approximately four feet above the bed and bolted to concrete blocks in front of the window in each cell. In its first opinion [(966 F.2d 606 (11th Cir. 1992)], the appeals court stated that "*it is true that prison officials are not required to build a suicide-proof cell. By the same token, however, they cannot equip each cell with a noose.* It falls to the plaintiff on remand to establish that defendants were deliberately indifferent to the probability that inmates would attempt to commit suicide by hanging themselves from the bar."

In the second opinion, after an *en banc* review of the first decision, the court overturned the verdict by stating that the prior history of suicides did not show that "all prisoners of the Jefferson County Jail are substantially likely to attempt suicide." In the midst of this prolonged litigation, the defendants covered up the pipes in question, as well as updated its intake screening and staff training policies.

2) *Natriello v. Flynn* [837 F. Supp. 17 (D. Mass. 1993) and 36 ATLA L. Rep. 368 (Dec. 1993)]. In *Natriello*, the 19-year-old decedent was incarcerated in a county jail in January 1989. During the intake assessment, he reported a prior history of IV drug use, a suicide attempt, family history of both suicidal behavior and substance abuse, and the recent death of his grandfather. The decedent was also suffering from hepatitis. During seven months of incarceration, he engaged in aggressive, combative and self-destructive behavior resulting in both disciplinary confinement and observation under suicide watch. On August 18, 1989, the decedent engaged in self-destructive behavior, was transported to the local hospital for treatment of injuries, and subsequently returned to the jail and again placed under suicide watch. Less than two days, he was found hanging from a ceiling grate in his cell by a bed sheet. The medical examiner later determined that the decedent had been dead for approximately five to seven hours prior to being found.

During the jury trial, the plaintiff offered evidence that the two officers assigned to the unit housing the decedent on suicide watch were either laying down and/or sleeping in the control booth with the lights out for the majority of their shift. In addition, the officers were not supervising the activities of an "inmate watcher," who was assigned to sit in a folding chair in the corridor and monitor the decedent as well as a second suicidal inmate in an adjacent cell during an eight-hour shift. The inmate watcher allegedly left his post unattended after three hours. In addition, evidence was offered to suggest that suicide prevention policies and staff training were grossly inadequate, and that cells designated to house suicidal inmates were dangerous. The jury returned a verdict in favor of the plaintiff. In lieu of appeal, both sides subsequently agreed to a negotiated settlement of approximately $230,000.

3) *Heflin v. Stewart County* [958 F.2d 709 (6th Cir. 1992)]. A deputy went to the decedent's cell on September 3, 1987 and saw a sheet tied to the cell bars. The deputy immediately went to the dispatcher's office, told the dispatcher to call the sheriff and ambulance service, picked up the cell block keys, and returned to open the cell. When the deputy entered the cell, he observed the decedent "hanging by the neck

on the far side of the shower stall." The decedent's hands and feet were tied together, a rag was stuffed in his mouth, and his feet were touching the floor. With the body still hanging, the deputy checked for a pulse and signs of respiration, but found none though the body was still warm. He also opened the decedent's eyes and found the pupils were dilated. From these observations the deputy concluded that the decedent was dead. While the deputy was still alone in the cell with the hanging body, a jail trusty arrived with a knife he had picked up in the kitchen. Rather than utilize the knife to cut the decedent down, the deputy ordered the trusty out of the area. The sheriff arrived shortly thereafter and directed the deputy to take pictures of the decedent before he was taken down.

At trial, the plaintiffs introduced evidence that the defendant maintained a policy of leaving victims as discovered, despite the medical procedures available to resuscitate victims. They ultimately prevailed and a jury awarded damages to the decedent's family based upon proof that the defendants' acted with deliberate indifference after discovering the decedent hanging. The defendants appealed by arguing that the decedent was already dead and their action or inaction could not have been the proximate cause of his death. The appeals court ruled that "there clearly was evidence from which the jury could find that Heflin died as the proximate result of the failure of Sheriff Hicks and Deputy Crutcher to take steps to save his life. They left Heflin hanging for 20 minutes or more after discovering him even though the body was warm and his feet were touching the floor...The unlawfulness of doing nothing to attempt to save Heflin's life would have been apparent to a reasonable official in Crutcher or Hick's position in 'light of pre-existing law'..." The court also affirmed the award of damages in the amount of $154,000 as well as approximately $133,999.50 in attorney fees.

See also *Tlamka v. Serrell* [8th Circuit, No. 00-1648, March 2001], in which the court ruled that three correctional officers could be sued for allegedly ordering inmates to stop giving CPR to an inmate who collapsed in a prison yard following a heart attack. The court stated that "any reasonable officer would have known that delaying Tlamka's emergency medical treatment for 10 minutes, with no good or apparent explanation for the delay, would have risen to an Eighth Amendment violation."

4) *Simmons v. City of Philadelphia* [947 F.2d 1042 (3rd Cir. 1991)]. The decedent was arrested for public intoxication and transported to a police precinct lockup for "protective custody." He was initially described by the arresting officer as being heavily intoxicated, agitated, and crying. During the first few hours of incarceration, the booking officer periodically observed the decedent as having "glassy eyes...in a stupor" with behavior ranging from confusion to hysteria. The booking officer subsequently discovered the decedent hanging from the cell bars by his trousers. He was cut down and paramedics were called, but the booking officer did not initiate any life-saving measures. The plaintiff filed suit alleging that the city violated the decedent's constitutional right to due process "through a policy or custom of inattention amounting to deliberate indifference to the serious medical needs of intoxicated and potentially suicidal detainees." At trial, the plaintiff offered evidence which showed that from 1980 through 1985, the city's police department experienced 20 suicides in its lockups, did not provide suicide prevention training to its officers nor intake screening for suicide risk to its inmates, or any other suicide prevention measures.

In affirming the jury verdict, the appeals court stated that "the evidence of 20 jail suicides in the Philadelphia prison system between 1980-85, of whom 15 were intoxicated, *the City's possession of knowledge before 1981 that intoxicated detainees presented a high risk of suicide, its awareness of published standards for suicide prevention, and its failure to implement recommendations of experts, including its own director of mental health services for the prison system, was sufficient basis for the jury to have found the unnamed officials with responsibility over the City's prisons acted recklessly or with deliberate indifference, thereby contributing to the deprivation of constitutional rights of plaintiff's decedent. If a city cannot be held liable when its policy makers had notice of a problem and failed to act, then it is difficult to posit a set of facts on which a city could be held liable to have been deliberately indifferent.*" The ruling also affirmed the lower court award of over $1.1 million in wrongful death, survival damages, and delayed damages to the plaintiff.

5) ***Cunningham v. Tkadletz*** [97 C 1109, Federal District Court for the Northern District of Illinois, 1998] Natiera Cunningham, 18-years-old, was arrested for misdemeanor offenses arising out of an alleged shoplifting incident. She was subsequently transferred to, and incarcerated in, the Gurnee, Illinois police lockup. Natiera was held on the misdemeanor charges, as well as on an outstanding felony warrant from Waukegan, Illinois. Shortly before midnight the same day she was arrested, Natiera attempted to commit suicide in the Gurnee lockup by preparing to hang herself with an article of clothing. Gurnee police, who maintained video surveillance of prisoners in their lockup, observed her and immediately intervened, preventing the suicide. Natiera was transported to a nearby hospital, briefly examined, and returned to the custody of the Gurnee police. Hospital discharge instructions directed that Natiera be placed on a "suicide watch," which was maintained by the Gurnee police for the duration of the night.

Waukegan Police Department Detective Mark Tkadletz spoke by telephone with a Gurnee police commander the next morning. After being apprised of Natiera's suicide attempt some 9 hours earlier, he drove to Gurnee to take custody of Cunningham for the purpose of interrogating her regarding the outstanding felony charge. Two Gurnee police commanders later testified at trial that Detective Tkadletz was informed in detail of Natiera's earlier attempted suicide and was apprised that her mother was concerned that she would attempt suicide again. The commanders advised Detective Tkadletz that they considered Natiera to be at continued risk of attempting to commit suicide.

Detective Tkadletz took custody of Natiera and transported her to the Waukegan Police Department. While at the police station, he interrogated the young woman regarding the pending felony charge for approximately 30 minutes during which, by his own report, she became increasingly upset, and ultimately stopped answering his questions. Detective Tkadletz subsequently took Natiera to court for a bond hearing. He never relayed any of the information he received concerning Natiera's suicide attempt or her continuing risk of suicide to court deputies, or to anyone else.

Natiera was remanded to the Lake County Jail in Waukegan. Laarni Dazal, a nurse for Correctional Medical Services (CMS), a private contractor providing medical and mental health services at the facility, administered a suicide risk screening form on Natiera. The form consisted of a series of questions and observations. The answers given were recorded on a form and tallied to provide a numerical score. CMS regulations provided that a score of eight or higher required an immediate psychiatric referral. Although Natiera scored an "eight" on the form, Nurse Dazal failed to make a psychiatric referral or otherwise notify the jail authorities that the inmate might be suicidal. In a subsequent affidavit, the nurse stated she failed to make a psychiatric referral because she did not believe the truthfulness of some of Natiera's answers, i.e., her score was not a "legitimate eight." Accordingly, Natiera was not afforded any psychiatric treatment and was placed in the general jail population, without benefit of any type of suicide watch, or other precautions.

During her confinement, Natiera became increasingly frustrated and agitated over the inability of her family to raise money to bond her out of jail. For the next two days, she made repeated calls home, to no avail. At approximately 9:00 am on the morning of June 6, Natiera was told she was not scheduled to go to court or to be released that day. She became "disruptive" and was placed on 23-hour lock down by Erica Sandahl, a Lake County correctional officer working on the housing tier to which Natiera was assigned. Officer Sandahl returned to the housing tier from lunch at approximately 12:15 pm. Former inmates who testified at trial stated that Natiera had refused to eat her lunch that day, and had been pleading from her cell for someone to speak to. Other plaintiff witnesses testified that, while Natiera was calling out for help, Officer Sandahl remained in the day room watching a soap opera with inmates who were not on lock down. There was, however, no testimony offered at trial to suggest that Officer Sandahl had been told anything about Natiera having attempted suicide or expressing any desire to harm herself. At the end of the television program, the officer went to Natiera's cell and found her hanging from an overhead sprinkler. Emergency medical assistance was called. Shortly thereafter, Natiera Cunningham was pronounced dead at a nearby hospital.

In his trial testimony, Detective Tkadletz admitted he was informed of Natiera's earlier suicide attempt, but adamantly denied he was told that there was any continuing concern that the young woman remained at risk of suicide. The detective further maintained that since Natiera had been "treated and released" at a hospital, he was fully justified in concluding there was no reason to believe that she was at continued risk of committing suicide. He maintained, therefore, there was no need for him to have informed the sheriff's deputies of Natiera's suicide attempt the previous night. Detective Tkadletz also maintained that Natiera did not "appear suicidal" or "depressed," and testified that her demeanor was similar to that of other arrestees with pending felony charges.

*A settlement of all claims against Correctional Medical Services and Nurse Dazal was arrived at in advance of trial. The claim against Officer Sandahl was dismissed by the trial judge at the conclusion of the plaintiff's evidence. On October 28, 1998, an eight-person jury returned a verdict in favor of the plaintiffs and against Detective Tkadletz, totaling $1,350,000, including $750,000 in punitive damages.*

6) *Jacobs v. West Feliciana Sheriff's Department* [WL 1289478, 5th Cir., 2000]. On August 21, 1996, Sheila Jacobs was arrested for the attempted, second-degree murder, by shooting, of her uncle. Jacobs had become enraged at her uncle when she learned that he had allegedly sexually molested one of her sons years before. The arresting state troopers informed an investigator for the West Feliciana Sheriff's Department that Jacobs told them shortly after her arrest that, after shooting her uncle, she had tried to kill herself by placing a loaded gun in her mouth and pulling the trigger, but the gun had jammed. The investigator conveyed this information to Sheriff Bill Daniel and Deputies Earl Reech and Wayne Rabalais.

After processing Jacobs, the officers at the West Feliciana Parish Prison placed Jacobs in a "detox" cell. According to Deputy Rabalais, when Jacobs was placed in the detox cell, the officers had her on suicide watch and had placed a note to that effect in the control center. Although a portion of the detox cell could be observed from the jail's control room through a window, a substantial amount of the cell (including the bunk area) fell into a "blind spot" and was not visible from the control room. This cell could be completely observed only if an officer viewed it from the hallway. The cell also had several "tie-off" points (bars and light fixtures from which a makeshift rope could be suspended), despite Sheriff Daniel's acknowledgment that a suicide prevention cell should not have such tie off points and despite the fact that another inmate (James Halley) had previously committed suicide in the very same cell by hanging himself with a sheet from one of these tie-off points. To the best of Deputy Rabalais's knowledge, and pursuant to Sheriff Daniel's directive, Jacobs was not given sheets on the first night of her detention, August 21.

On the morning of August 23, an attorney visited Jacobs at the jail. He requested that Sheriff Daniel leave Jacobs in the detox cell, and perhaps provide her with a blanket and towel. Sheriff Daniel instructed one of his deputies to give these items to Jacobs, but the record reflects only that Jacobs received a sheet (which she eventually used to kill herself), and there is no evidence that she received either a towel or a blanket.

Deputies Earl Reech and Rabalais were on duty at the West Feliciana jail facility from 11:30 p.m. the night of August 23, until 7:30 a.m. the next morning, August 24, 1996. The record reveals that the defendants still regarded Jacobs as a suicide risk during that time. Indeed, Sheriff Daniel testified that Jacobs was on a "precautionary," though not a "straight" suicide watch. Our review of the record reveals few discernible differences between these two types of suicide watches. When an inmate was on "strict" suicide watch, the informal policy at the jail was to have the inmate checked on every fifteen minutes. Deputy Reech testified that he and Deputy Rabalais made periodic checks on Jacobs; however, it is unclear exactly how often the deputies checked on Jacobs while she was under the "precautionary" suicide watch. What is clear is that as many as 45 minutes elapsed from the time a deputy last checked on Jacobs to the time she was discovered hanging from the light fixture in the detox cell.

Specifically, the record reveals that, after having observed Jacobs in the detox cell at 12:22 a.m. and 1:00 a.m., Deputy Reech checked on Jacobs at 1:22 a.m., and he observed her lying awake in her bunk. At 2:00 a.m., Deputy Rabalais went to investigate some loud music down the hall, and on his way back to the control station, he observed Jacobs lying awake in her bunk. Deputy Rabalais testified that both he and Deputy Reech checked on Jacobs sometime between 2:00 and 2:44 a.m., and that Jacobs was still awake in her bunk. After this last check, Deputy Reech returned to the jail lobby to read his newspaper. At approximately 2:44 a.m., Deputy Rabalais looked into the detox cell from the control room and saw what appeared to be part of an arm hanging from the ceiling. Concerned, he went to find Deputy Reech, who was still reading the newspaper, to help him get into the detox cell. When the deputies arrived at the cell, they found Jacobs hanging from a sheet that had been tied around the caging surrounding a ceiling light fixture. Deputy Rabalais found a knife and enlisted the assistance of another inmate in cutting the sheet and lowering Jacobs onto the floor. By all indications, Jacobs had torn a small string from the bunk mattress and wrapped that string around the sheet to form a make-shift rope. The paramedics who arrived only moments later were unable to resuscitate Jacobs. Jacobs's suicide was the third suicide at the jail during Sheriff Daniel's tenure there. As noted above, James Halley's suicide had occurred in the same cell where Jacobs killed herself. The third suicide had occurred in a cell down the hallway from the detox cell. The family of Sheila Jacobs filed suit.

On September 13, 2000, the United States Court of Appeals for the 5th Circuit ruled that the family had sufficient grounds to sue then-Sheriff Bill Daniel and Deputy Rabalais. The court stated, in part, that:

"The record before us reveals that Sheriff Daniel was aware that Jacobs had tried to kill herself once before and that she posed a serious risk of trying to do so again. Throughout the time Jacobs was in the jail, Sheriff Daniel considered her to be a suicide risk. Under Sheriff Daniel's supervision, Jacobs was placed in the detox cell, which had a significant blind spot and tie-off points, despite the fact that during Sheriff Daniel's tenure another detainee, James Halley, had committed suicide in the same cell by hanging himself from one of the tie-off points....Moreover, Sheriff Daniel ordered his deputies to give Jacobs a blanket and towel, despite the fact that he still knew that she was a suicide risk. He did not offer any reason for doing so other than Jacobs's appointed counsel's suggestion that she be given these items, and in fact, he acknowledged that a suicidal person should not have loose bedding of any kind in a cell with them. Sheriff Daniel also acknowledged that it was not advisable to place a suicidal detainee in a cell with tie-off points, even though the detox cell had tie-off points. We note also that with full awareness that a prior suicide occurred in the detox cell by way of an inmate securing a blanket to a tie-off point therein, Sheriff Daniel did nothing to eliminate or conceal the tie off points in the detox cell, which cell Sheriff Daniel's own unwritten policy mandated as the appropriate cell for housing suicidal detainees....*We would find it difficult to say that this behavior could not support a jury finding that Sheriff Daniels acted with deliberate indifference, and likewise we find it even more difficult to say that this conduct was objectively reasonable.* For these reasons, as well as for substantially the same as those reasons given in the Magistrate Judge's order denying summary judgment, we affirm the denial of qualified immunity for Sheriff Daniel as to claims asserted against him in his individual capacity....

....Deputy Reech was the senior deputy on duty when Jacobs killed herself. Like Sheriff Daniel and Deputy Rabalais, he had actual knowledge that Jacobs was a suicide risk at all times during her detention. He also knew about the earlier hanging suicide of James Halley in the detox room, and with respect to the Halley and Jacobs suicides, Reech deposed that there was nothing they (at the jail) could do to stop the detainees from killing themselves if they wanted to and that it wasn't their responsibility. Despite this knowledge, and the fact that nothing had been done to correct either the blind spot or the tie-off points in the detox cell, Deputy Reech ordered Jacobs to be placed in it for a suicide watch. Like Sheriff Daniel, Deputy Reech was on notice that these facilities were 'obviously inadequate'....

....We note that it was Sheriff Daniel, not Deputy Reech, who made the decision that Jacobs be given a blanket. The fact that Reech did not make the decision that Jacobs should have a blanket would seem to militate in favor of finding qualified immunity, since after all, if no blanket had ever been provided, it would not have made any difference which cell he had placed her in. On the other hand, Deputy Reech did observe Jacobs lying on the bunk in the detox cell several times during the period when she had the sheet, and despite his awareness that a prior suicide occurred in the detox cell using a blanket and that suicidal inmates should not be given lose bedding, he did not take the sheet away from Jacobs. Additionally, Deputy Reech did not check on Jacobs as frequently as he was supposed to....

....Given Deputy Reech's level of knowledge about the significant risk that Jacobs would attempt to harm herself and his disregard for precautions he knew should be taken, we conclude that there is enough evidence in this record from which a reasonable jury could find subjective deliberate indifference. And in light of Deputy Reech's failure to insure that adequate precautions were taken to protect Jacobs from her known suicidal tendencies, we find that Deputy Reech's conduct falls outside the realm of that which could be characterized as being objectively reasonable in light of the duty to not act with subjective deliberate indifference to a known substantial risk of suicide....

....We conclude that no reasonable jury could find that Deputy Rabalais, who had only been on the job for about six months at the time of Jacob's death, acted with deliberate indifference, and we further find that his conduct, in light of the record evidence, was objectively reasonable, thus entitling him to qualified immunity from suit in his individual capacity. While Deputy Rabalais, like his co-defendants, had actual knowledge that Jacobs was a suicide risk at all times during her confinement, he did not make the decision to place her in the detox cell. As noted above, Deputy Reech, the senior deputy on duty with over twenty years of experience, made that decision. Deputy Rabalais likewise had nothing to do with the order that Jacobs be given a blanket and towel, which order was evidently interpreted by some unknown jail official as entitling Jacobs to a loose sheet instead....

....The only element of Jacobs's detention over which Deputy Rabalais had direct control was the frequency with which he checked on her. Like Deputy Reech, Deputy Rabalais did not comply with Sheriff Daniel's unwritten policy of checking on Jacobs every fifteen minutes. However, this failure to abide by Sheriff Daniel's policy alone evinces at best, negligence on the part of Deputy Rabalais, which is insufficient to support a finding of deliberate indifference....

....As a result of the foregoing analysis, we dismiss this appeal as it relates to the official capacity claims asserted against Sheriff Daniel for a lack of interlocutory appellate jurisdiction, we affirm in part the Magistrate Judge's order to the extent that it denies summary judgment on grounds of qualified immunity on the individual capacity claims asserted against Sheriff Daniel and Deputy Reech, and we reverse in part the Magistrate Judge's order to the extent it denies summary judgment on grounds of qualified immunity on the individual capacity claims asserted against Deputy Rabalais and we remand to the district court for entry of judgment in his favor."

# LIABILITY FOR JAIL AND PRISON SUICIDE: A CASE STUDY[1]

On April 17, 1996, Nancy Bloom, 17-years-old, was arrested on various charges (including threatening her mother with a knife) and incarcerated in the West County Jail. Thirty days later on May 17, she committed suicide. Her family later sued the county, the private medical provider, and individual jail and mental health staff.

The civil complaint, filed in federal court, contained numerous allegations that the defendants were either negligent and/or deliberately indifferent to Nancy Bloom, resulting in her death. The allegations included inadequate supervision levels for inmates, "dangerously low correction officer staffing," and subjecting Nancy Bloom to "cruel and barbaric conditions." The Complaint also alleged that jail officials and staff deliberately ignored Ms. Bloom's suicidal behavior and medical condition, and that mental health staff deliberately withdrew her psychotropic medication.

Upon intake into the facility on April 17, 1996, Ms. Bloom was booked and processed by Officer Thelma Bruin. Officer Bruin completed various paperwork, including a Suicide Prevention Screening Guidelines form. Officer Bruin interviewed Ms. Bloom and made several notations on the form, including that she had a psychiatric history, previous suicide attempts, and showed signs of depression. According to Officer Bruin, the inmate was initially laughing and unconcerned about her predicament but began to "tear up" when asked about any prior history of suicide. Because of this behavioral change, together with information contained on the court's commitment order noting Ms. Bloom's "past emotional and psychiatric difficulties (including suicidal ideations, two psychiatric hospitalizations, on-going psycho-therapy (sic), and her dependence upon the psychotropic drug 'Zoloft' as an anti-depressant and suicide preventative...", Officer Bruin made a referral for further assessment to mental health staff. In fact, Officer Bruin photocopied the commitment order and hand-carried the document over to a nurse in the intake area of the jail. In addition, this information was entered into the facility's computer system for access by mental health staff.

As a result of this referral, Ms. Bloom was assigned to B-Block (the women's section of the facility's mental health unit) and placed on "close watch." One officer is assigned to this 25-cell block. Jail staff documented the close watch order in the B-Block Security Log. The close watch was terminated by Frank Garth, a social worker, following an assessment of Ms. Bloom on the morning of April 18, 1996. The following day (April 19) Ms. Bloom was assessed by Lynda Boseman, Ph.D., a clinical psychologist. Although she was cleared for "general population" by Dr. Boseman, jail staff decided to house Ms. Bloom in the mental health unit throughout the remainder of her incarceration.

---

[1]This case study was compiled by Lindsay M. Hayes. In order to ensure complete confidentiality, the names of the victim, facility, and staff have been changed. No other modifications to the facts of this case have been made.

# EXECUTIVE SUMMARY

**Seminar: Correctional Health Care: Suicide Prevention   01-P603**

June 25 - 28, 2001

**National Institute of Corrections - Prisons Division**

# Correctional Health Care: Suicide Prevention

## Table of Contents

CRITICAL ISSUES . . . . . . . . . . . . . . . . . . . . . . . . . . . . . . . . . . . . . . . . . . . . . . . . . . . . . . 2

THE ATTITUDE OF PREVENTION . . . . . . . . . . . . . . . . . . . . . . . . . . . . . . . . . . . . . . . 4

DEFINITIONS . . . . . . . . . . . . . . . . . . . . . . . . . . . . . . . . . . . . . . . . . . . . . . . . . . . . . . . . 8

RESEARCH AND STATISTICS . . . . . . . . . . . . . . . . . . . . . . . . . . . . . . . . . . . . . . . . . . 9

PROVIDING A HOLISTIC APPROACH USING STANDARDS OF CARE . . . . . . . . . . . . . 10

LIABILITY ISSUES IN PRISON SUICIDE . . . . . . . . . . . . . . . . . . . . . . . . . . . . . . . . . . . 14

BEING PREPARED FOR CRISIS INTERVENTION . . . . . . . . . . . . . . . . . . . . . . . . . . . 16

SHORT TERM TREATMENT . . . . . . . . . . . . . . . . . . . . . . . . . . . . . . . . . . . . . . . . . . . 18

AFTERCARE . . . . . . . . . . . . . . . . . . . . . . . . . . . . . . . . . . . . . . . . . . . . . . . . . . . . . . . 19

SPECIAL POPULATIONS . . . . . . . . . . . . . . . . . . . . . . . . . . . . . . . . . . . . . . . . . . . . . . 20

AFTERMATH OF A SUICIDE . . . . . . . . . . . . . . . . . . . . . . . . . . . . . . . . . . . . . . . . . . . 26

ACTION PLANNING . . . . . . . . . . . . . . . . . . . . . . . . . . . . . . . . . . . . . . . . . . . . . . . . . 28

## Correctional Health Care: Suicide Prevention
## Critical Issues for Suicide Prevention

On June 26 - 28, 2001, a seminar titled, "Correctional Health Care: Suicide Prevention," was held at the National Institute of Corrections Academy in Longmont, Colorado. The following consultants gave presentations:

- Lance Couturier, Ph. D., Pennsylvania Department of Corrections

- Teena Farmon, Criminal Justice Consultant

- Lindsay M. Hayes, Assistant Director of the National Center on Institutions and Alternatives

- Frederick R. Maue, M.D., Pennsylvania Dept. Of Corrections, Chief of Clinical Services

- Bonita M. Veysey, Ph. D., Assistant Professor and Director of the Center for Justice and Mental Health Research at Rutgers University, School of Criminal Justice

The workshop was coordinated by Madeline Ortiz, Program Coordinator for the National Institute of Corrections, Prisons Division. This document was compiled by Renee Bergeron, Staff Development and Training consultant.

Twenty four participants attended the seminar. The participants were from the United States, Guam, and the Mariana Islands.

### CRITICAL ISSUES

The participants were asked "What do you believe to be the three most pressing issues facing prisons in managing suicide?" The issues identified were:

#### Staff Training
It is difficult to have an accessible, portable yet engaging and useful suicide prevention training for all staff.
#### Policies and Procedures
There is a lack of detailed policy and procedure regarding suicide prevention.

## Resources (Staffing and Funding)

Legislative appropriation for new positions is very important, yet it can be difficult to obtain. Funding can affect the quality/number of staff, the physical plant and the quality of care that can be provided.

## Team Concept

There is a need to have and use a shared language. Medical staff need to learn the operations lingo and corrections officers and administrators need to learn the mental health language. There must be shared responsibility of all aspects of suicide prevention (policy development, implementation, and review.)

Training is another issue connected to the team concept. It is critical to use a team approach to conduct training.

## Early Identification

We must make the switch from looking at diagnosis to looking at risk factor information. This ties into sharing and standardizing data between organizations and eliminating redundancy.

## Communication

Communication among staff and the public is critical. So many things create barriers to success such as cultural and political issues. Good communication can help reduce the barriers. Set expectations for communication (i.e., cooperative communication among different areas is expected).

## Clinical Issues

Having adequate assessments and the trained and skilled staff to categorize inmates is a critical issue. It is critical to provide assessment and treatment for those inmates with no mental health history that are a suicide risk.

You have identified issues critical to you. Our goal in this seminar is to provide you with some ideas to address these issues as well as to provide an opportunity to share ideas among yourselves.

# THE ATTITUDE OF PREVENTION

**Lindsay M. Hayes**

To begin, I want you to think of suicide prevention as a process, a continuum of services. What do you do when you have a suicide attempt? How do you successfully manage to make sure that it does not re-occur? How do you turn paper policy into action?

One of your critical issues was the need for team work. You are right! Suicide prevention is a collaborative effort. It is not an issue for just prison administrators, health care professionals, or custody staff, it is an issue for all institutional staff.

Let's examine some guiding principles that need to be used when considering suicide prevention.

You mentioned that one obstacle to successful suicide prevention is "communication." Communication needs to begin "at the top." What we are talking about is communication in the very broad sense in that it includes the "attitude" of the communication. The administrator drives the policy, practice, and the attitude of staff. The administrator sets the tone for the way the institution will operate.

In my research and experience I have found that negative attitudes often impede meaningful prison suicide prevention efforts. Such attitudes form obstacles to prevention and can be seen on both a local and universal basis. Simply stated, obstacles to prevention are empty excuses that inmate suicides can not be prevented. So what are some obstacles to achieving the desired attitude?

Here are some examples of obstacles I have actually heard (or heard about) in my work:

- We did everything we could to prevent this death, but he showed no signs of suicidal behavior.

- There is no way you can prevent suicides unless you have someone sitting watching the prisoner all the time, and no one can afford to be a baby sitter.

- We didn't consider him suicidal, he was simply being manipulative and I guess it just went too far.

- We aren't mind readers nor trained to be psychiatrists.

- If someone really wants to kill themselves, there's generally nothing you can do about it.

- Suicide prevention is a medical problem, it's a mental health problem, it's not our problem.

A successful suicide prevention program relies on a multi-disciplinary team, another critical issue you listed. Practice team building with staff to increase the success of your suicide prevention program. Team building involves regular, multi disciplinary meetings. These meetings help to foster a different mentality, they help staff to shift their paradigms (change their attitudes).

Then there are universal obstacles to prevention, regressive attitudes that are far more dangerous because of their far-reaching ability to negatively influence correctional policy on a larger scale. We often find the roots of this attitude in the world of academia:

- Statistically speaking, suicide in custody is a rare phenomenon, and rare phenomena are notoriously difficult to forecast due to their low base rate. We cannot predict suicide because social scientists are not fully aware of the casual variables involving suicide.

- Demographic profiles of custodial suicide victims are of little value for prediction because they often mirror the characteristics of typical jail or prison inmates.

- Even those skilled mental health professionals who have the time for extensive personal interaction with troubled individuals, either cannot forecast suicide or are unable to prevent patient suicide even if it had been somewhat anticipated.

- Jail and prison suicides are extremely difficult to predict due to their spontaneous nature.

- To speak bluntly, custodial suicide may constitute less a readily solvable problem than a situation which, in view of our present knowledge and our financial limitations, may be expected to continue.

So how do we change or defuse these local and universal obstacles?

I am not suggesting that any one of these quotes are incorrect but by espousing such beliefs, you are "setting yourself up" for your own protection rather than true prevention. If you have an attitude of true prevention ("I will not allow a suicide to occur in my facility." "I won't allow staff to be hurt.") you will have greater chance of success. The best suicide prevention plans, procedures and policies will not translate into action without the supporting "attitude."

For example, with over 5,000 inmates, the Orange County Jail System in Santa Ana, California, is the 12th largest jail system in the country, and 3rd largest in California. During the past 10 years, over 831,040 persons have been processed through the system and only 5 inmates have successfully committed suicide. The suicide rate in the Orange County Jail System is 9.4 deaths per 100,000 inmates versus the national rate of 107 per 100,000 inmates. Why? Because of the attitude. For example the jail commander has said:

"When you begin to use excuses to justify a bad outcome, whether it be low staffing levels, inadequate funding or physical plant concerns, (issues we struggle with each day) you lack the philosophy that even one death is not acceptable. If you are going to tolerate a few deaths in your correctional system, then you've already lost the battle."

This is an important kind of attitude. Not every suicide is preventable but the attitude of prevention begins at the top.

**Teena Farmon**

I bring to you the perspective of a prison administrator. I had thirty years of prison experience. I came into the system believing that suicide prevention was not a custody issue. But I can now share with you that, yes, it must be a concern of prison administrators. The Mental Health/Medical staff really might prefer us to stay out of it but litigation today shows that we clearly won't reduce the number of suicides or subsequent lawsuits unless we work together, as a team.

So, "what's in it for me?" Why should you in your role as Prison Administrator be interested in a holistic suicide prevention initiative. A holistic, solid suicide prevention program will:

- Increase safety of staff/inmates
- Reduce disruption in operations
- Improve risk management capability
- Reduce liability

**Safety of Staff**
Limiting the number of times our staff has to rush in and be exposed to body fluids or the inmate population reaction is going to increase their safety.

### Safety of Inmates
Inmate exposure to bodily fluids of other inmates and inmate potential physical reaction. The less times you have suicide attempts, the less times this will occur.

Inmates and staff are affected by the suicide of another inmate. The reaction tends to be magnified in a female institution or if the inmate attempting or committing the suicide is a popular inmate or an older inmate who has been in the institution for a long time.

An attempted or successful suicide may also increase the will of other inmates to complete potential suicide.

### Reduce Disruption in Operations
Inmate suicide can cause significant disruptions in every day operations. Frequently we must lock down the prison. We need to use all investigative staff to determine if it was suicide or murder. Inmate reactions often contribute to/cause the major operational disruption. Inmates are waiting to see how we respond. Did we do up front what we should have done? Do we show that we care about the situation? Did we understand all of the potential signals?

Who spends most of the time with inmates? Sure, Correctional Officers. So who needs to understand signs and symptoms of suicide? Yes, Correctional Officers but also inmates, teachers, food service workers, work supervisors. The inmates are spending a lot of time with these groups. Therefore, they all need to be educated in signs and symptoms and reporting processes.

You may come to work with your day planned but a suicide will certainly change that. Now you must respond. Headquarters, the media, and inmate family responses must be handled. If you have processes and procedures in place and you know them, you are in good shape. Responses such as, "I don't know" or "I don't think so," are not going to help your career.

### Improve Risk Management Capability
Prison Managers must be prepared to respond to risk management issues following a suicide. This means protect your assets, reduce your risk to liability. Someone is going to be checking behind you. Risk Management means to always assess what you have done and based on that assessment, determine where you need to go, what future action should be taken.

### Reduced Liability
As Prison Managers you may be personally liable for a suicide that occurs in your prison. In California a San Quentin warden was subject to a personal liability judgement. The law had to be changed to allow the state to pay the damages. Aside from personal liability, your

professional liability can certainly be damaged if suicides and suicide attempts frequently occur.

## DEFINITIONS

**Dr. Bonita M. Veysey**

Let's review some definitions relating to suicidal behavior.

**Self-Injurious Behavior (SIB)**
Any intentional act that results in organ or tissue damage to an individual, regardless of motivation or "mental state." This includes self-mutilation.

Often a building of intense, acute dysphoria that cannot be resolved non-destructively. The SIB is non dysphoria resolving.

**Para-suicidal Behavior**
An apparent attempt at suicide, as by self-poisoning or self-mutilation, in which death is not the desired outcome.

Suicide can be looked at as a grid.

### Level of Injury by Purpose

|  | Accidental | No Death | Death |
|---|---|---|---|
| **Minor Injury** |  | Self-harm Para-suicide | Suicide attempt |
| **Serious Injury** |  | Self-harm Para-suicide | Suicide attempt |
| **Death** |  | Suicide | Suicide |

When the intent is not to cause death (self injury, self mutilation), when there can be an assessment of intent it is important to assess the level of intent.

When there is a completed act we need to consider it a suicide, even if it may not have been intentional.

When death is intended (and not achieved) we need to attend to this in great depth.

Sometimes an individual might keep putting themselves in intentional danger and the reasons aren't clear.

### Self injury
Some people self injure for personal gain but there are other reasons for self injury. Women will self injure when they have a history of abuse, it has to do with connecting with self. Being able to do something to know that you are there, so the self injury is about self recognition. We often believe that this is a way they manipulate the system but it is not, it is about them trying to feel (something, anything).

### Issues of Severity and Intent
Severity, how do you determine what constitutes a significant attempt? It is very hard. For example, is a small cut to the wrist serious? Is taking six aspirins serious? Once you have determined what constitutes a significant attempt you create a liability issue. What happens when you are wrong?

### Necessary Components for Successful Suicide
In any suicide three things must come together in time and space for a suicide to happen.

1. Inmate must have the WILL. Most prevention programs focus on changing the will.

2. Inmate must have the OPPORTUNITY. The inmate must be alone and unobserved or else the suicide will be interrupted. Research has shown that it is better NOT to isolate those who threaten suicide attempts.

3. Inmate must have the MEANS to commit the suicide. The canteen can be a cornucopia of "means." Extension cords and Tylenol are often available in the canteen and can be used to commit suicide.

If you can disrupt any of these three things than suicide prevention can be effective. This can include additional cell observation or reducing access to means, etc. For successful suicide prevention, think beyond changing just the inmate's will. Think about medication, staffing issues etc. In some jurisdictions inmates are trained to be observers and actually paid for this duty. This approach must be carefully monitored but the benefit is that it can reduce suicides in a facility.

# RESEARCH AND STATISTICS

## Lindsay M. Hayes

To give you a perspective of the difference between prison and jail suicides here are some fast facts from some research done from 1984 - 1993. (Unfortunately, there has not been an updated, nation wide research effort since 1993). There is however a periodic newsletter, *Jail Suicide/Mental Health Update*. (A joint project of the National Center on Institutions and Alternatives and the National Institute of Corrections, U.S. Department of Justice). The Summer 2000 issue is included in Attachment 1.

### Jails

- There are over 400 jail suicides (excluding prisons) each year, and suicide is the leading cause of death in jails through out the country.

- The rate of suicide in county jails is estimated to be 107 deaths per 100,000 inmates or a rate that is approximately 9 times greater than in the community.

- Most jail suicides occur within the first 24 hours of incarceration; most victims were isolated from both staff and inmates and not screened for potential suicidal behavior at intake. **Note:** *This is a generalization that will vary from jurisdiction to jurisdiction.*

### Prisons

- There are over 160 prison suicides each year, and suicide is the third leading cause of death in prisons, behind natural causes and AIDS.

- The rate of suicide in prisons is estimated to be between 15 and 17 deaths per 100,000 inmates or a rate that is approximately 20 - 25 percent greater than in the community.

- The majority of prison suicide victims had documented histories of mental illness and suicidal behavior; many victims were housed in administrative segregation at the time of their deaths.

An analysis of total prison suicides by state over a thirteen year period (1984 - 1997) indicates that there has been a systematic reduction in the number of suicides since 1984. (In 1984 the rate was 27.1. In 1997 the rate was 15).

# PROVIDING A HOLISTIC APPROACH USING STANDARDS OF CARE

## Lindsay M. Hayes

The purpose of a suicide prevention and response program is to establish standards of intervention response and to minimize inmate suicide rates.

Correctional standards are in general, advisory and voluntary unless a federal judge tells you to comply. The three resources for standards that relate to suicide prevention are: The National Commission on Correctional Health Care(NCCHC), the American Correctional Association (ACA), and the American Psychiatric Association (APA).

NCCHC standards on suicide prevention suggest a 12 step protocol that includes identification, training, and assessment. (See Attachment 2). The APA includes suicide prevention standards that are identical to NCCHC standards. The current ACA standard is general and does not provide much guidance.

## ACA Standard 3-4364 - Suicide Prevention and Intervention
*There is a written suicide prevention and intervention program that is reviewed and approved by a qualified medical or mental health professional. All staff with responsibility for inmate supervision are trained in the implementation of the program.*

***Comment:*** The program should include specific procedures for intake screening, identification, and supervision of suicide-prone inmates.

## Policy and Procedure
If you choose to use a set of standards your internal policies must be consistent with these standards. Inconsistencies will sometimes occur in cases where you contract with an outside entity for services. When you write or revise policy remember that it is important to be consistent.

All correctional facilities, regardless of size, should have a detailed written suicide prevention policy that addresses the following critical components. You may notice that several of the components are the same as the critical issues you mentioned such as: training; communication; identification and screening; and intervention. This information should give you a few ideas for addressing these critical areas.

## TRAINING

**Staff Training**: All correctional, medical, and mental health staff should receive eight hours of initial suicide prevention training, followed by two hours of annual training. Training should include why correctional environments are conducive to suicidal behavior, potential pre-disposing factors to suicide, high-risk suicide periods, warning signs and symptoms, and components of the facility's suicide prevention policy.

Curriculum must engage and involve staff. It must address attitudes (towards inmates/suicide in general). Training must be much more than reading and initialing policy, it must include adequate practice during the training and refreshed with practice drills every few months.

Remember we talked about the importance of attitude earlier. It is important in training that you grab the staff or inmates attention immediately with that prevention attitude.

**Dr. Lance Couturier**

**Inmate Training**: The Pennsylvania Department of Corrections has developed a video to educate inmates about suicide signs and symptoms. The video was a collaborative project at the institution that included inmates and a variety of custody and treatment staff. The video is available in English and Spanish.

The video project was a result of a suicide. The Pennsylvania Department of Corrections had previously been distributing a brochure on suicide prevention ("Living Through it - Suicide Prevention for People in Prison," also available in English and Spanish) but not all of the inmates could read. So, to better reach every inmate, the video was made. In the video, inmates are advised where to obtain help in the facility if they are experiencing emotional distress. They are encouraged to watch out for the welfare of other inmates and advised to make referrals to mental health staff if they observe some of the symptoms of depression and other mental health problems. (*Jail Suicide/Mental Health Update*, Summer 2000)

**Lindsay M. Hayes**

## IDENTIFICATION AND SCREENING

Intake screening for suicide risk must take place immediately upon confinement and prior to housing assignment. This process may be contained within the medical screening form or as a separate form, and must include inquiry regarding: past suicidal ideation and/or attempts; current ideation, threat, plan; prior mental health treatment/hospitalization; recent significant loss (job, relationship, death of family member/close friend, etc.); history of suicidal behavior by family member/close friend; suicide risk during prior contact/confinement with agency; and arresting/transporting officer(s) believes inmate is currently at risk. The process must include procedures for referral to mental health and/or medical personnel.

There is an example of an intake screening tool ("Suicide Risk Indicators Checklist for RH/SMU") in *Jail Suicide/Mental Health Update*, Summer 2000 on page.4.

## COMMUNICATION
Develop procedures that enhance communication at three levels: Between the arresting/transporting officers(s) and jail staff; between and among jail staff (including medical and mental health personnel); and between jail staff and the suicidal inmate.

## HOUSING
Housing must be based on needs and classification. Isolation should be avoided. Whenever possible, house in the general population, mental health unit, or medical infirmary, located in close proximity to staff. Inmates should be housed in suicide resistant, protrusion free cells. Removal of an inmate's clothing (excluding belts and shoelaces), as well as use of physical restraints (e.g. handcuffs, straitjackets, leather straps etc.) should be avoided whenever possible, and only utilized as a last resort for periods in which the inmate is physically engaging in self-destructive behavior. These decisions should be made in collaboration with medical and/or mental health staff.

Many systems just have one option for housing inmates classified with mental health issues, restrictive housing units.

It is not advisable to have "non-medical" staff conduct mental health assessments. It could open you up to lawsuits.

Emergency placements will need to occur but you need to follow up with a complete assessment as soon as possible.

I want to take a minute to share a "report card" on state standards and prison suicide prevention I published in 1995 for the National Institute of Corrections (*Prison Suicide: An Overview and Guide to Prevention*. Washington, D.C.: National Institute of Corrections U.S., Department of Justice.) Think about where your organization stands in comparison.

- 79% of prison systems had a suicide prevention policy
- 15% did not have a policy but had some protocols in other policies
- 6% of prison systems did not address the issue of suicide prevention at all
- 52% addressed the issue of staff training
- 75% addressed the issue of housing
- 79% addressed the issue of supervision, but the highest level of supervision varied considerably:
    - 34% listed constant watch

- 44% listed 15 minute watch
- 20% listed 5 to 10 minute watch
- 2% listed 30 minute watch

- 23% addressed the issue of intervention
- 27% addressed the issue of mortality review

## LIABILITY ISSUES IN PRISON SUICIDE

There are two roads to the courthouse: Tort suit and civil law suit.

**Tort Suit**
This claim alleges only that the defendant was negligent in a way which caused, or failed to prevent, the suicide. A tort suit seeks only damages.

**Civil Rights Action**
This claim, brought pursuant to 42 USC Section 1983, alleges that a person, acting under color of state law, violated or acted with "deliberate indifference" in causing a violation of the decedent's constitutional rights. A civil rights action can seek both compensatory and punitive damages, as well as injunctive relief.

Today, there is a lot of information published about suicide prevention. Twenty years ago this was not the case. Years ago administrators might have been able to claim that they didn't know how to go about preventing suicide. Today a correctional administrator does not have an excuse for not having suicide prevention policies and training established within his or her facility. Additionally, these policies and training must reflect current "standard correctional practice," meaning it must be similar to what other jurisdictions are doing. Failure to establish and follow these protocols can be considered deliberate indifference.

**Deliberate Indifference**
- Has been defined as "apathy of unconcern."
- Has been defined as conduct that is below malicious or sadistic but higher than malpractice or negligence.
- Has been defined as "criminal recklessness" or a conscious disregard of a high risk of harm.
- It has been a very "jail-friendly" legal standard in litigation of jail suicides.

**Negligence**
What about being negligent, what does that mean? It is anything that results in a harm that

doesn't involve deliberate indifference. For example, not complying with policy that results in an injury is an example of negligence. It rises to the level of deliberate indifference when it is a "pretty outrageous" case. For example, an inmate has attempted to kill him or her self using clothing. The staff doesn't take away clothing and the inmate then successfully kills him or her self using the clothing. This could be deliberate indifference. To avoid a case of deliberate indifference you need to make sure that you don't go "outside the scope of your employment."

Here is a summary of a case on deliberate indifference: In Farmer v. Brennan [114 S.Ct. 1970 (1994)], the U.S. Supreme Court has further refined "deliberate indifference" by using the subjective standard ("actual knowledge"), rather than the objective standard ("ought to have known"):

> We hold instead that a prison official cannot be found liable under the eighth amendment for denying an inmate humane conditions of confinement unless the official knows of and disregards an excessive risk of inmate health and safety; the official must be aware both of facts from which the inference can be drawn that a substantial risk of serious harm exists, and he must also draw the inference .......
>
> ...... We doubt that a subjective approach will present prison officials with any serious motivation to take refuge in the zone between "ignorance of obvious risk" and the "actual knowledge of risks" .... A fact finder may conclude that a prison official knew of a substantial risk from the very fact that the risk was obvious. ....
>
> .... For example, if an eighth amendment plaintiff presents evidence showing that a substantial risk of inmate attacks was "longstanding, pervasive, well-documented, or expressly noted," by prison officials in the past, and the circumstances suggest that the defendant-official being sued has been exposed to information concerning the risk and thus "must have known" about it, then such evidence could be sufficient to permit a trier of fact to find that the defendant-official had actual knowledge of the risk ....
>
> .... The question under the eighth amendment is whether prison officials, acting with deliberate indifference, exposed a prisoner to a sufficiently substantial "risk of serious damage to his future health" ... and it does not matter whether the risk comes from a single source or multiple sources, any more than it matters whether a prisoner faces excessive risk of attack for reasons personal to him or because all prisoners in this situation face such a risk....

> ...... Prison officials who actually know of a substantial risk to inmate health or safety may be found free from liability if they responded reasonably to the risk even if the harm ultimately was not averted ...

In interpreting Farmer, a plaintiff attorney in prison suicide cases will try different strategies including:

**Individual v. Generalized Risk**: Using the Farmer language of it does not "matter whether the prisoner faces an excessive risk of attack for reasons personal to him or because all prisoners in his situation face such a risk," they will argue that certain inmates belong to identifiable groups known to be vulnerable and this generalized risk renders jailers deliberately indifferent when they fail to take reasonable preventive measures.

Repeated examples of negligence might rise to deliberate indifference: A plaintiff attorney might argue that deliberate indifference might occur following repeated examples of negligence which disclose a pattern of conduct by prison staff. While a single act viewed in isolation might appear to be the product of negligence, repeated examples of such treatment bespeak a deliberate indifference by officials or staff.

Television monitoring can come back to haunt you if you have not followed procedure. For example, if you have an inmate hanging for 20 minutes with no response by correctional staff during that 20 minutes, you are probably going to lose the subsequent law suit.

Response time is an essential issue but sometimes different policies are conflicting. One policy might state that immediate response is required and another policy might state that a cell entry response team is required to enter the cell. So, as I mentioned earlier, make sure that your policies are congruent and don't conflict.

**Note:** Attachment 3, *Jail and Prison Suicide Litigation: Case Law Review*, provides case summaries of significant jail and prison suicide litigation (compiled by Mr. Hayes).

## BEING PREPARED FOR CRISIS INTERVENTION

**Teena Farmon**

Suicide intervention is the clinical and organizational response to a suicide attempt. The primary goals are to prevent death and stabilize the individual.

**Emergency Protocol**
One of the things we often do is use phrases that we believe meet some generic definition and we expect staff to be aware of critical things that have not been clearly described or defined as expectations. For example, telling staff to report "bizarre" behavior, what does "bizarre behavior" mean? How is staff supposed to ascertain what is bizarre and what is not? Not only do you need to clearly outline expectations and definitions during training, you need to make sure that the processes are as simple as possible. Post orders should be very specific and detail manual activities that must occur. When writing or reviewing policy ask the question, "Would the staff member, without any other assistance or training, be able to accomplish what you want them to do?" Your training should of course, follow your protocol.

Emergency protocol should include procedures for:

- Summoning medical assistance
- Maintaining life support (in a suicide intervention program your goal is to avoid death, preserve life)
- Providing routine practice of Emergency Response Drills
- Universal precautions - In California, universal precaution standards requires people to "suit up" into jump suits, protective gloves, masks, booties, etc. How much time passes while someone is "suiting up"? How does that impact our ability to preserve life? You need to have your policy allow for staff to make independent decisions based on individual situations. There may be times they need to enter the cell without the "suit." I suggest that officers carry gloves and mouth guards attached in a pouch on their belt at all times. (A poll of participants indicated that this was done in most of their organizations.)

Establishing emergency protocols:

- **Decide who has on-site responsibility**. Do your protocols identify who is the on-site supervisor at the time of the incident? In a medical emergency, are your protocols clear?

- **Decide who may access/enter the cell/unit**. What if your policy says, "You will not enter a cell without back up"? You are alone and discover an inmate hanging in a cell. Do you leave them hanging while waiting for back-up because that is policy? What if it turns out that the inmate is faking it and it is a trap? How would it be to go to court and say that you allowed an inmate to hang while you waited for back up to arrive?

The American Correctional Association Standards require a four minute maximum response time. (Medical research shows that brain damage occurs within that time frame in a hanging situation.) It is our responsibility as an organization to put into place a system that allows a sufficient number of staff to get into that cell within that time.

- **Equipment.** What equipment is required in response to a medical emergency? Examples are cut down kits, a Stokes litter, or crash carts. Can the staff handle the equipment? Can the physical plant accommodate the equipment?

- **Use of mechanical restraints.** Who has the authority to authorize mechanical restraints?

- **Transportation.** What are expectations? Medical/custody staff often don't understand what issues are involved in transportation from one location to another. For instance if someone has a compound fracture, medically, it wouldn't be a good idea to move them.

## SHORT TERM TREATMENT

**Dr. Bonita M. Veysey**

The soles purpose of short term treatment is to stabilize the individual after a suicide attempt.

- **Behavioral controls**
  Mechanical restraints - physical control of individuals. The positive aspect of using mechanical restraints is that you restrict an individuals harm to self and others. Some negative consequences are the emotional impact. Research in Massachusetts shows a reduction in the incidence of seclusion and restraints. This was accomplished by asking questions on intake to a Psychiatric unit. Upon admission, the patients were asked, "What are the things that cause you to act out, the things that trigger your violent or destructive behavior? When you are like that, what helps you to calm down?"

  Some responses were: "being able to talk with someone"; "being able to pound a pillow"; and "being able to be alone." Next they are told: "If you are out of control and we have to restrain you, here are your choices; medication, restraint chair, or three point restraints. If we have to use those devices, what would you prefer?" This open dialogue between you, who has control, and the inmate, helps to reduce the need right up front for mechanical restraints. These intake files created upon admission to the

Psychiatric Unit are now a permanent record and are used into the future. If a suicide attempt does occur, the crisis team secures the individual and uses the inmates preferred method of restraint.

This can help the inmates get control of themselves emotionally. You may be able to work out behavioral plans and controls that can reduce the incidence of suicide attempts and disruptive events.

- **Formularies**
   One of the single largest cost in corrections is medications (first HIV medications and second Psychiatric medications). What kinds of controls do you have over what medications are in your pharmacy? How are they prescribed? How are they distributed? These are processes to consider and address when writing suicide prevention protocol.

## AFTERCARE

**Dr. Fred Maue**

Aftercare in terms of suicide prevention means the care we provide for an offender once he or she is stabilized following a suicide attempt. The trend is to use the least restrictive restraints for the least amount of time possible. One option used is "open seclusion" where the inmate is put into an open room to quiet down with officer observation.

Treatment plans need to take into account what the staff are feeling about the inmate. We need to not only meet the needs of the inmate but we must also consider staff needs. Meeting staff needs can directly relate to improvement in the inmate behavior. The inmate's behavior will improve if the staff are interested in helping them to improve.

What about inmates who attempt suicide for non-mental health reasons? How can you manage them? What do you do with them? One strategy is to try to determine the "why." Why does an inmate want to go to administrative segregation? Because they can smoke? Privacy?

Some of this group are your "untreatable" inmates. What do you do with "untreatable" inmates? One strategy is to move them around (to other facilities or sections of your facility) to give staff a break. But you need to maintain a level of consciousness when doing this to make sure you don't abuse the strategy. The custody staff aren't the only ones who burn out, it is also the mental health staff that need a break.

This is another opportunity to look at things holistically, from an organizational view point. In order to provide adequate, quality treatment we must also treat our staff appropriately. Always consider, "What is best for the inmate, the other inmates in the unit and the staff?"

Getting people on suicide watch doesn't seem to be particularly difficult but getting them off can be. In these cases once you move them back (or begin the process to move them back) they threaten suicide again. This type of inmate is usually being manipulative and does not have mental health issues. Their interest is more likely reassignment to a certain institution, a place to smoke, a way to stay out of the main population etc.

So if is not a mental health issue. What can you do?

Participant discussion included ideas such as:

- Have a mental health staff person state, "This inmate is not an imminent suicide risk. We will attempt to treat the inmate on the (standard housing) unit. The mental health staff will see the inmate, but will see him/her in his/her regular residence."

- Conduct an in depth assessment.

- Wait for the inmate to do something and then let the mental health staff intercede.

- Put the inmate on special observation when they are first returned to the (standard housing) unit. For example, a 15 minute watch for 72 hours.

The critical thing is to make sure you have follow up care after someone is stabilized and off of suicide watch.


## SPECIAL POPULATIONS

### Teena Farmon

There is an array of special needs inmates within each of our facilities. Some examples include: female, non-English speaking, geriatric, disabled, mentally ill, hospice, and youthful offender inmates. Each of these populations has a special set of needs. As an administrator you need to recognize these special populations and their needs and address it in your policies. Let's take a look at each of them in a little more detail.

### Non English speaking

We live and work in a culturally diverse population and need to be aware of how those differences impact how we operate. In some cultures, for example, you have to be aware of the different emotional issues relating to someone who attempts suicide. Also, non-English speaking inmates present a significant issue if there are no staff to translate. You need to have staffing that reflects the diversity that exists in your population.

In California, staff were paid an additional 5% for being bi-lingual. Part of their job was to be on call for emergency translation. For scheduled events such as hearings, outside vendors were hired to provide interpretation.

### Disabled

Accommodations must be made for the physically, hearing and visually impaired.

### Developmentally Disabled

This group of inmates are those with learning disabilities or the inability to read or write. Many institutional systems house the developmentally disabled within their mental health units.

### Youthful Offenders

States have varying policies regarding this group.

### Dr. Bonita M. Veysey

### Females

You need to adjust your operating procedures when working with female populations. Let me illustrate why with two true and sadly typical stories.

## "Healing to Hope, Hoping to Heal"

**Maria** was 42, had 3 children, and was sexually abused by her father from about age 6 through 11 years. She was both physically and emotionally abused. She ran away as a young teenager. Her drug of choice was cocaine. She was involved in prostitution, multiple relationships, and a victim of violence during many of these relationships. (Violence in the life of female inmates tends to be vast and pervasive.) She attended some substance abuse treatment but was not interested in giving up her drugs. Once released from treatment, she returned to drug use. In her 30's, after losing custody of her children, she began to take treatment more seriously. At the same time, the facility she was in and out of started to change the way they treated women (women were now being treated as a unique population).

Maria began to explore the "why's" of what she was doing. She realized she could say no to violence. In the facility the staff had finally stopped asking, "What is wrong with you?" and started to ask " What is happening with you?"

Her last time in prison, prior to her suicide attempt, Maria was positive she was going to make it. She moved to a safe neighborhood and had an enjoyable job in a professional office. Three months later she got bored and started using cocaine again. Six months later she was re-incarcerated. She asked the pod supervisor for a razor. The facility had curtains. She slit her throat from ear to ear.

She was saved. The first thing she said when awakening in the hospital was "How deep do I have to cut?"

**Sheila** was 24 years old. She had been arrested and jailed twice. Abused as child, she was very frightened in the facility. She became easily agitated. She was diagnosed with depression and on medication. When agitated, she rocked to soothe herself. This rocking behavior concerned the staff (because they didn't understand why she was doing it). They took action and moved in on her, to stop her. Sheila became more agitated and started banging her head. The staff call the Special Operations team to come in and forcibly take Sheila to the mental health unit to calm down.

The staff in the mental health unit recognized that Sheila's rocking was related to the violence she had experienced as a child. Rocking helped her to reconnect with self. The mental health staff was able to put together a behavioral plan to look at what she and the staff would do when she became agitated.

As a result of this incident, the facility changed procedures. Now, the Special Operations Unit is on hand, but staff talk to the inmate first.

When children are abused it is usually by someone the child must rely on such as a parental figure or a friend of the family. This is a situation the child can't escape. To deal with it, the child fractures or disassociates. Their perception of reality becomes warped. During a violent incident the child learns to act like a rabbit, freeze, become passive. Because children have to believe in their parents they blame themselves. As they grow up, they run away, they abuse substances. The behaviors that saved them as children don't work as adults, they get labeled as "symptoms" such as "borderline personality disorder." How treatable is that? They are hopeless, angry, and manipulative. What are the treatment options?

If I told you that many of these women are actually experiencing Post Traumatic Stress Disorder (PTSD) overlaid on depression versus "borderline personality disorder," how would that change your reaction? Yes, you can actually treat PTSD and depression.

There is an entire field around the issues of women and trauma emerging. Findings indicate that to successfully treat these females: you must address substance abuse, you may never be able to eliminate hyper-vigilance or disassociation but you can help these women recognize symptoms and understand what is happening to them. Treatment needs to be holistic and based in relationships. You have to talk about their reactions to trauma.

Successful treatment works to "re-contexualize" the past. "The things that happened were indeed terrible, but you were a victim and not to blame." The women must work to create new identities of self. The women must be given opportunities to assume new, meaningful roles. They must transform their identity from mental health patient, to survivor to a current occupational title.

Those are some ideas about what to do with your female population. Here are some thoughts about what not to do. Don't recreate situations that remind the women of (their past) abuse (it can be smells, sounds, and sights). When we reduce womens options either by not communicating important information or taking away their ability to have control over their bodies, it is dangerous. Typical policies and procedures can heighten a women's anxiety. If she rocks (to self soothe) and we tell her to stop, we block her coping mechanisms. The woman may then act out in rage or attempt suicide as a response.

I ask you to consider how you respond to women in critical incidents and imagine how your response seems to a woman who was raped or beaten as a child. A woman might be terrified of being in the dark and alone, being tied down, or being unclothed. If your crisis response team is mostly men, you need to reconsider your staffing. This can be terrifying and may reproduce the same visceral feelings of childhood abuse.

If you can make some of these small changes you will have specific, concrete payoffs. It can reduce the injury to the female offenders and staff. It can reduce hospital stay length and future incidents.

**Dr. Fred Maue**

**Geriatric Population**
Individuals age 65 and older are the fastest growing age group in America. Correctional systems are also experiencing the aging of their inmate population. The number of inmates 55 years and older doubled in the nine year period from 1981 to 1990. From 1985 to 1997,

one-third of the state correctional systems experienced over a 400 percent increase in their age 50 plus inmate population.

The concern stems from this populations need for long term care. Long term care refers to both personal care (also known as assisted living) and skilled care. Personal care means that the inmate maintains his independence and performs tasks with minimal assistance. The inmate can no longer function in the general population of the prison environment. The inmate typically requires verbal cues and prompting.

Skilled care means the inmate is routinely supervised by licenced personnel to provide individual nursing care, related medical, and other health services in a 24 hour period. The inmate is unable to care for him or her self.

Here are some unique and important facts about elderly inmates:

- Due to their medical and social histories, i.e. drug use, high risk sexual behavior, smoking and neglect of health, inmates' may have a medical age 5 to 10 years older than their chronological ages.

- The cost of incarcerating this population is about three times higher than that of other prisoners. The most expensive portion of this cost is health care.

- This population has special needs for housing, work assignments, social interaction, education (preparation for end of life), health care, self care, post release placement, and family interaction. Unfortunately, most correctional systems are not yet prepared to address these problems.

- Correctional staff in many states have limited training pertaining to the management of elderly inmates.

- There is not a consistent definition of geriatric or elderly inmates. Correctional systems typically designate the elderly population at age 50, 55, or 60. The National Institute of Corrections recommends using age 50 because of the poor health level of many older inmates.

- Some elderly inmates suffer from two to three chronic conditions while incarcerated. Common health conditions include hypertension, cardiac, diabetes, skeletal/locomotor and cognitive/intellectual problems.

Why the increase in elderly in prisons?

- Changes in laws such as "life with no parole," longer mandatory sentencing, and "three strike laws."

- Improved health care in the prison system.

- A trend in reduced Parole Board approvals for the release of sex offenders and violent offenders.

What are the correctional care management issues with this geriatric population? Questions the manager must ask (and answer based on his or her own specific facility), include:

- What kinds of support activities/services are needed?

- What managerial issues are raised?

- What are the implications for post-release planning and coordination with parole?

- Should efforts be made to provide alternative placement in the community or should the elderly and other long term care inmates serve their sentences in prison?

- What is the impact to prison work assignments, counseling, classification, education, and recreation activities?

As a manager, your goal should be to:

- Address all aspects of needs, particularly around health care services.

- Ensure appropriate accommodations. Long term care inmates should be assigned to facilities that provide the most suitable accommodations and environment by facilitating patient mobility and service delivery.

- Enhance care and interactions by establishing in-service training for facility staff.

- Use staff resources wisely.

To expand on the idea of using staff resource wisely: Inmate helpers can be trained to help with hospice care or other duties. The duties must be strictly supervised, limited in scope and specific, (Federal case law prevents inmates from providing medical care to other inmates). Examples of duties inmates may perform are: Push wheelchairs, help others get dressed, and help with showers.

What is the link between the geriatric patient, mental illness, and suicide risk?

- Mental illness plays an important role in 25 percent of suicides, and this percentage rises with age: From 50 percent in suicides who are over fifty years old to over 70 percent in suicides older than sixty.

- Most suicide attempts reflect a person's ambivalence about dying; patients requesting assisted suicide show an equal ambivalence. When interviewed two weeks after a request for assisted suicide, two-thirds of these patients show a significant decrease in strength of the desire to die.

- Like other suicidal individuals, patients who desire an early death during a serious or terminal illness are usually suffering from a treatable depressive condition. Although pain and other factors, such as a lack of family support, contribute to their wish for death, depression is the most important factor, and researchers have found it to be the only factor that significantly correlated with the wish for death.

- Suicidal patients are especially prone to setting absolute conditions on life such as: "I won't live .... without my husband, .... if I lose my looks, power, prestige, or health, or ..... if I am going to die soon." These patients are afflicted by the need to make demands on life that cannot be fulfilled. Determining the time, place, and circumstances of their death is the most dramatic expression of their need for control.

- Patients who attempt suicide and those who request assisted suicide often test the affection and care of others. Expressions such as, "I don't want to be a burden to my family," or "My family would be better off without me," usually reflect depressed feelings of worthlessness or guilt or may be a plea for reassurance. Not surprisingly, they are also classic indicators of suicidal depression in people who are in good physical health. Whether physically healthy or terminally ill, these individuals need assurance that they are still wanted; they also need treatment for their depression.

## AFTERMATH OF A SUICIDE

### Lindsey M. Hayes

Despite all our good efforts we have a suicide ..... now what?

- Reporting process/protocol: In the event of a suicide attempt or suicide, all appropriate officials should be notified through the chain of command.

- Following the incident, the victim's family should be immediately notified, as well as appropriate outside authorities. It is important to be available to the family after a suicide occurs. This can actually help prevent lawsuits by diffusing suspicions.

- All staff who came into contact with the victim prior to the incident should be required to submit a statement that includes their full knowledge of the inmate and incident. Their reports should be brief, accurate, and specific to personal knowledge of the incident and not what they assumed or thought happened.

- If logs were not filled out appropriately prior to the incident, NEVER try to "play catch up."

## Critical Incident Stress Debriefing (CISD)

"Responding to and/or observing a suicide in progress can be extremely stressful for staff and inmates. The plan should specify the procedures for offering a critical incident debriefing to all affected personnel and inmates." (NCCHC, 1997)

The Debriefing:

- Must be legitimate, not simply a paper policy. The administration must show employees that it cares about their future and that they are willing to support the CISD process.

- Can be either formal or informal and must be offered on a voluntary basis.

- Must be strictly confidential. It can not be associated with investigative or administrative review of the inmate's suicide, or issues of potential liability.

- Can be offered through the corrections department, employee assistance program, local mental health provider, or community CISD team. At least one member of the team should be a police officer, Emergency Medical Technician or someone who is used to responding to critical incidents.

- Should be held within 24 to 72 hours of the incident.

- Should provide affected staff with the opportunity to process their thoughts and feelings about the incident, create an understanding of critical stress symptoms, and develop ways of dealing with those symptoms (research shows that the CISD process usually takes from 2 to 4 hours).

- Should encourage staff to seek further assistance beyond the CISD process.

## Mortality Review

Every completed suicide, as well as suicide attempt that requires hospitalization, should be examined by a mortality review. The purpose of a mortality review is straight forward: What happened in the case under review and what can be learned to reduce the likelihood of future incidents?

The mortality review team must be multi-disciplinary and include direct care, mental health and medical personnel. Exclusion of one or more disciplines will severely jeopardize the integrity of the mortality review.

The mortality review, separate from other formal investigations that may be required to determine the cause of death, should include:

1. A critical review of the circumstances surrounding the incident.

2. A critical review of facility procedures relevant to the incident.

3. A synopsis of all relevant training received by involved staff.

4. Pertinent medical and mental health services and reports involving the victim.

5. Recommendations, if any, for change in policy, training, physical plant, medical or mental health services, and operation procedures.

Attachment 4 is a guide that can be used when conducting a mortality review. Notice that almost every major heading corresponds to the critical issues that you identified at the beginning of this seminar (training, identification, communication, etc.)

Polling of class participants revealed that in Louisiana the use of mortality reviews has lowered incidence of suicides.

Courts have requested copies of mortality reviews when sued in cases of suicide. You can be protected from turning over a mortality review in a lawsuit if you designate it a "quality assurance" document. Don't put the mortality review document in the medical file because it is then a public document and can be used in court.

## ACTION PLANNING

To conclude the, participants were asked how they planned to use the information from this seminar:

- Train Staff: I plan to develop training material to better train the staff on identification of suicidal risk. I plan to develop training for security staff on the developmentally disabled population. I plan to revise current suicide prevention training to include this material.

- Educate Inmates: I plan to make a video/develop a brochure to educate all inmates about suicide prevention. I plan to train select inmates on how to identify the signs and symptoms.

- Policy and Procedure: I will review related policy and procedure, review emergency response protocol. I will convene an interdisciplinary panel and immediately review our suicide prevention policy and procedures.

- Mortality Reviews: I plan to use the mortality review checklist. I will conduct my mortality reviews differently based on this information.

- Geriatric Suicide: I plan to look at geriatric needs and care required. I plan to examine the issues of long term care, particularly cost issues.

- Female Issues: I plan to think about our response protocols related to females and how they are handled related to suicide attempts. I have a new appreciation for the unique needs of female offenders in relation to suicide/attempted suicide. I will examine the way female inmates are treated and the specific ways they can be handled differently.

- Share Information: I will take the information back and share.

- Screening Tools: I plan to start using a Restricted Housing Unit screening tool.

- Critical Incident

    I plan to implement a process for CISD. I plan to conduct follow up after incidents to address Post Traumatic Stress Disorder.

- Diversity Issues: I see the need for making changes to address cultural issues as they relate to suicide risk/prevention.

- Tracking Systems: I see the need and plan to track inmates with a history of suicidal behavior. I plan to develop an in-house tracking system for inmates with suicidal behavior.

- Establish Communication Systems

    I see the need to establish better communication between medical and custody staff. I plan to improve overall communication between different staff in the institution. I like the idea of communication via interstate teleconferencing regarding inmate cases. I plan to use a clinical, medical and custody review team. I plan to consider new ways to include family members after a suicide death.

# ATTACHMENTS

1. *Jail Suicide/Mental Health Update*, National Center on Institutions and Alternatives and the National Institute of Corrections, U.S. Justice Department. Volume 9, Number 4 (Summer 2000).

2. NCCHC Standard J-53: Suicide Prevention (1997).

3. *Jail and Prison Suicide Litigation: Case Law Review*, prepared by Linsday M. Hayes.

4. *Mortality Review Guidelines*, Lindsay M. Hayes.

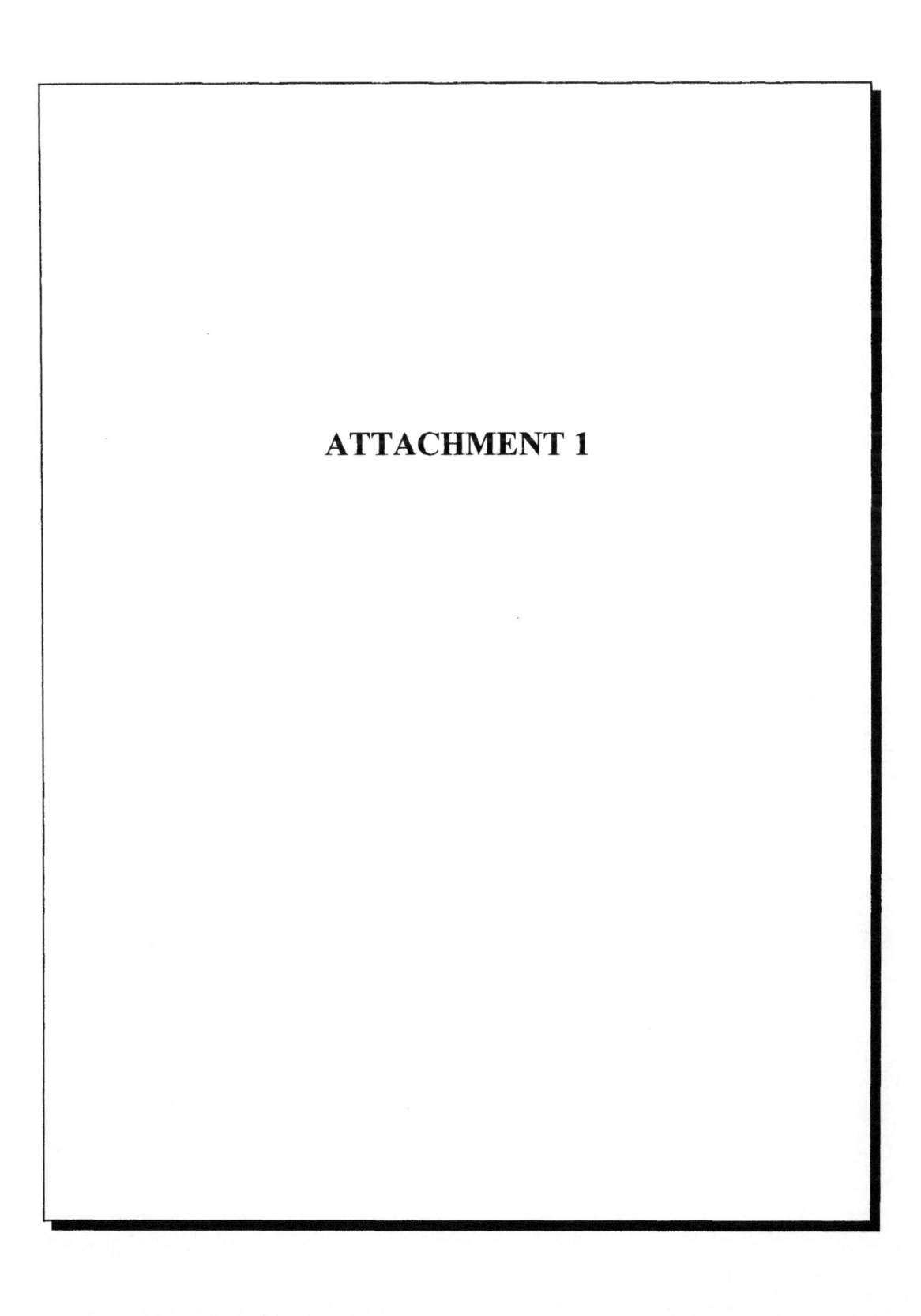

**ATTACHMENT 1**

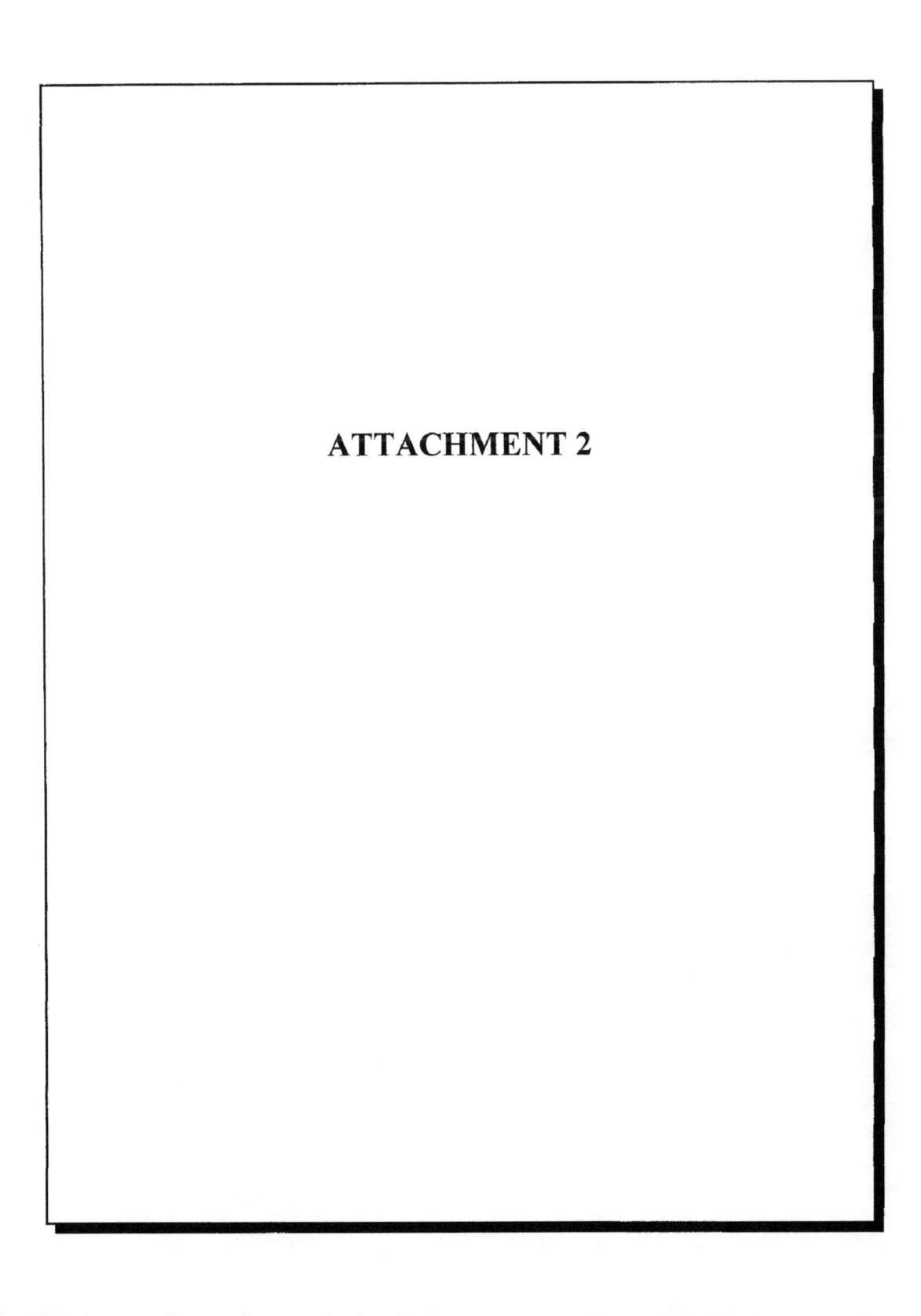

**ATTACHMENT 2**

# NCCHC Standard J-53: Suicide Prevention (1997)

Written policy and defined procedures require, and actual practice demonstrates, that the prison has a program for identifying and responding to suicidal inmates. The program components include training, identification, monitoring, referral, evaluation, housing, communication, intervention, notification, reporting, review, and critical incident debriefing.

**Discussion:** While inmates may become suicidal at any point during their stay, high risk periods include the time immediately upon admission to the prison facility; following new legal problems (e.g., new charges/additional sentence(s), institutional proceedings, denial of parole); following the receipt of bad news regarding self or family (e.g., serious illness or the loss of a loved one); and after suffering some type of humiliation or rejection (e.g., sexual assault). Inmates entering and/or unable to cope with administrative segregation or other specialized single-cell housing assignments are also at increased risk of suicide. In addition, inmates who are in the early stages of recovery from severe depression may be at risk as well.

Key components of a suicide prevention program include the following:

1. **Identification.** The receiving screening form should contain observation and interview items related to the inmate's potential suicide risk.

2. **Training.** All staff members who work with inmates should be trained to recognize verbal and behavioral cues that indicate potential suicide. The plan should include initial and subsequent training.

3. **Assessment.** This should be conducted by a qualified mental health professional, who designates the inmate's level of suicide risk.

4. **Monitoring.** The plan should specify the facility's procedures for monitoring an inmate who has been identified as potentially suicidal. Regular, documented supervision should be maintained.

5. **Housing.** A suicidal inmate should not be housed or left alone. An appropriate level of observation must be maintained. If a sufficiently large staff is not available that constant supervision can be provided when needed, the inmate should not be isolated. Rather, s/he should be housed with another resident or in a dormitory and checked every 10 - 15 minutes. An inmate assessed as being high suicide risk always should be observed on a continuing, uninterrupted basis or transferred to an appropriate health care facility. The room should be as nearly suicide-proof as possible (i.e., without protrusions of any kind that would enable the inmate to hang him/herself.)

6. **Referral.** The plan should specify the procedures for referring potentially suicidal inmates and attempted suicides to mental health care provider or facilities.

7. **Communication.** Procedures should exist for communication between health care and correctional personnel regarding the status of the inmate.

8. **Intervention.** The plan should address how to handle a suicide in progress, including appropriate first-aid measures.

9. **Notification.** Procedures should be in place for notifying jail administrators, outside authorities, and family members of potential, attempted, or completed suicides.

10. **Reporting.** Procedures for documenting the identification and monitoring of potential or attempted suicides should be detailed, as should procedures for reporting a completed suicide.

11. **Review.** The plan should specify the procedures for medical and administrative review if a suicide or a serious suicide attempt (as defined by the suicide plan) does occur.

12. **Critical incident debriefing.** Responding to and/or observing a suicide in progress can be extremely stressful for staff and inmates. The plan should specify the procedures for offering critical incident debriefing to all affected personnel and inmates.

**ATTACHMENT 3**

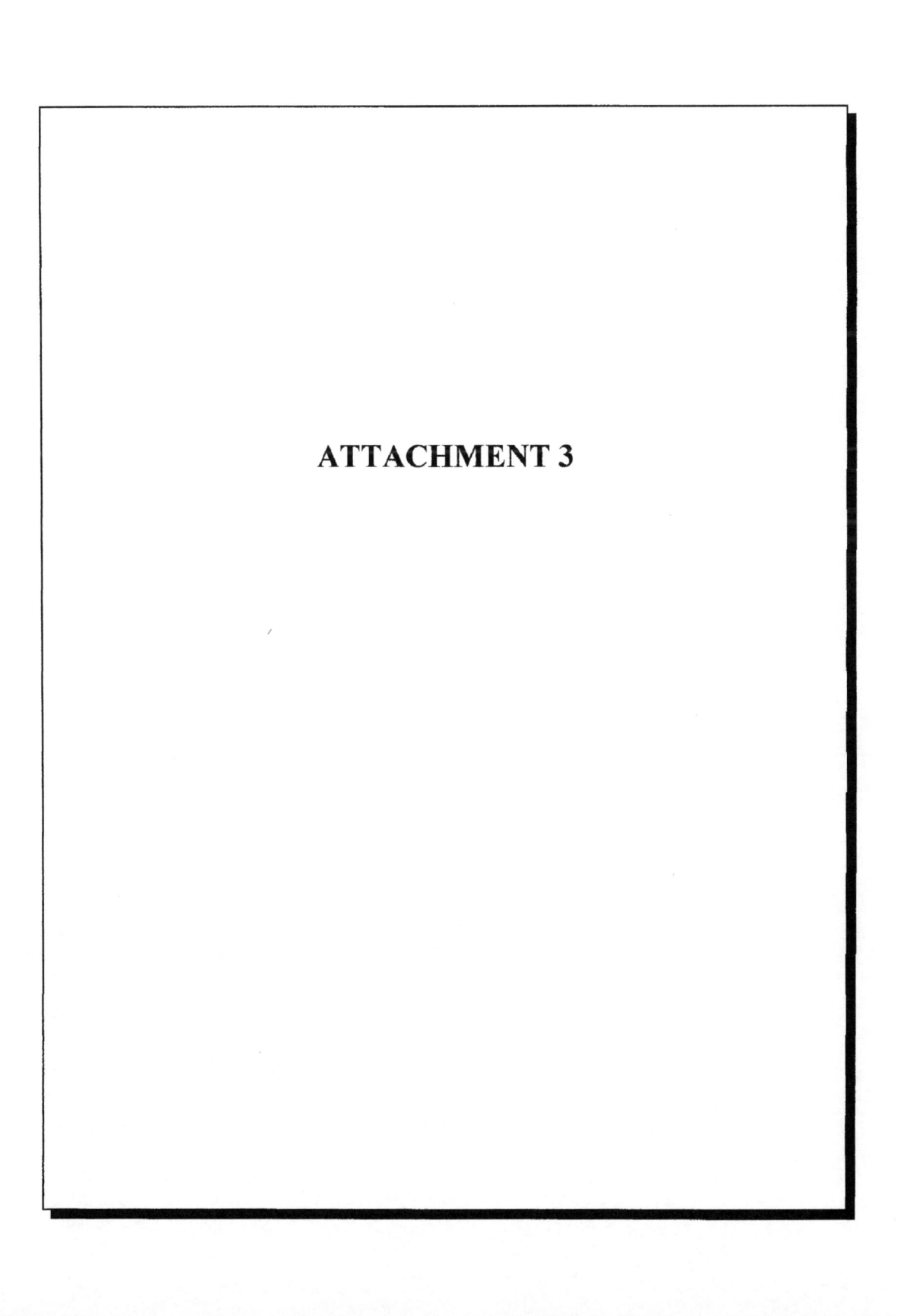

# JAIL AND PRISON SUICIDE LITIGATION: CASE LAW REVIEW

1. *Tittle v. Jefferson County Commission* [10 F. 3rd 1535 (11th Cir. 1994)]

2. *Natriello v. Flynn* [837 F. Supp. 17 (D. Mass. 1993) and 36 ATLA L. Rep. 368 (Dec. 1993)]

3. *Heflin v. Stewart County* [958 F.2d 709 (6th Cir. 1992)]

4. *Simmons v. City of Philadelphia* [947 F.2d 1042 (3rd Cir. 1991)]

5. *Cunningham v. Tkadletz* [97 C 1109, Federal District Court for the Northern District of Illinois, 1998]

6. *Jacobs v. West Feliciana Sheriff's Department* [WL 1289478, 5th Cir., 2000]

# JAIL AND PRISON SUICIDE LITIGATION: CASE LAW REVIEW

*Listed below are case summaries of significant jail and prison suicide litigation compiled by Lindsay M. Hayes. This listing is not intended to be all inclusive. Revised May 2001.*

1) ***Tittle v. Jefferson County Commission*** [10 F. 3rd 1535 (11th Cir. 1994)]. Between October 1987 and December 1989, 57 suicide attempts occurred in the county jail, including four successful suicides within the 12-month period of September 1988 and 1989. The majority of these incidents involved hangings from various window bars or pipes in the facility. Each pipe, measuring six inches in diameter and filled with concrete, was located approximately four feet above the bed and bolted to concrete blocks in front of the window in each cell. In its first opinion [(966 F.2d 606 (11th Cir. 1992)], the appeals court stated that "*it is true that prison officials are not required to build a suicide-proof cell. By the same token, however, they cannot equip each cell with a noose.* It falls to the plaintiff on remand to establish that defendants were deliberately indifferent to the probability that inmates would attempt to commit suicide by hanging themselves from the bar."

In the second opinion, after an *en banc* review of the first decision, the court overturned the verdict by stating that the prior history of suicides did not show that "all prisoners of the Jefferson County Jail are substantially likely to attempt suicide." In the midst of this prolonged litigation, the defendants covered up the pipes in question, as well as updated its intake screening and staff training policies.

2) ***Natriello v. Flynn*** [837 F. Supp. 17 (D. Mass. 1993) and 36 ATLA L. Rep. 368 (Dec. 1993)]. In *Natriello*, the 19-year-old decedent was incarcerated in a county jail in January 1989. During the intake assessment, he reported a prior history of IV drug use, a suicide attempt, family history of both suicidal behavior and substance abuse, and the recent death of his grandfather. The decedent was also suffering from hepatitis. During seven months of incarceration, he engaged in aggressive, combative and self-destructive behavior resulting in both disciplinary confinement and observation under suicide watch. On August 18, 1989, the decedent engaged in self-destructive behavior, was transported to the local hospital for treatment of injuries, and subsequently returned to the jail and again placed under suicide watch. Less than two days, he was found hanging from a ceiling grate in his cell by a bed sheet. The medical examiner later determined that the decedent had been dead for approximately five to seven hours prior to being found.

During the jury trial, the plaintiff offered evidence that the two officers assigned to the unit housing the decedent on suicide watch were either laying down and/or sleeping in the control booth with the lights out for the majority of their shift. In addition, the officers were not supervising the activities of an "inmate watcher," who was assigned to sit in a folding chair in the corridor and monitor the decedent as well as a second suicidal inmate in an adjacent cell during an eight-hour shift. The inmate watcher allegedly left his post unattended after three hours. In addition, evidence was offered to suggest that suicide prevention policies and staff training were grossly inadequate, and that cells designated to house suicidal inmates were dangerous. The jury returned a verdict in favor of the plaintiff. In lieu of appeal, both sides subsequently agreed to a negotiated settlement of approximately $230,000.

3) ***Heflin v. Stewart County*** [958 F.2d 709 (6th Cir. 1992)]. A deputy went to the decedent's cell on September 3, 1987 and saw a sheet tied to the cell bars. The deputy immediately went to the dispatcher's office, told the dispatcher to call the sheriff and ambulance service, picked up the cell block keys, and

returned to open the cell. When the deputy entered the cell, he observed the decedent "hanging by the neck on the far side of the shower stall." The decedent's hands and feet were tied together, a rag was stuffed in his mouth, and his feet were touching the floor. With the body still hanging, the deputy checked for a pulse and signs of respiration, but found none though the body was still warm. He also opened the decedent's eyes and found the pupils were dilated. From these observations the deputy concluded that the decedent was dead. While the deputy was still alone in the cell with the hanging body, a jail trusty arrived with a knife he had picked up in the kitchen. Rather than utilize the knife to cut the decedent down, the deputy ordered the trusty out of the area. The sheriff arrived shortly thereafter and directed the deputy to take pictures of the decedent before he was taken down.

At trial, the plaintiffs introduced evidence that the defendant maintained a policy of leaving victims as discovered, despite the medical procedures available to resuscitate victims. They ultimately prevailed and a jury awarded damages to the decedent's family based upon proof that the defendants' acted with deliberate indifference after discovering the decedent hanging. The defendants appealed by arguing that the decedent was already dead and their action or inaction could not have been the proximate cause of his death. The appeals court ruled that "there clearly was evidence from which the jury could find that Heflin died as the proximate result of the failure of Sheriff Hicks and Deputy Crutcher to take steps to save his life. They left Heflin hanging for 20 minutes or more after discovering him even though the body was warm and his feet were touching the floor...The unlawfulness of doing nothing to attempt to save Heflin's life would have been apparent to a reasonable official in Crutcher or Hick's position in 'light of pre-existing law'..." The court also affirmed the award of damages in the amount of $154,000 as well as approximately $133,999.50 in attorney fees.

See also *Tlamka v. Serrell* [8th Circuit, No. 00-1648, March 2001], in which the court ruled that three correctional officers could be sued for allegedly ordering inmates to stop giving CPR to an inmate who collapsed in a prison yard following a heart attack. The court stated that "any reasonable officer would have known that delaying Tlamka's emergency medical treatment for 10 minutes, with no good or apparent explanation for the delay, would have risen to an Eighth Amendment violation."

4) *Simmons v. City of Philadelphia* [947 F.2d 1042 (3rd Cir. 1991)]. The decedent was arrested for public intoxication and transported to a police precinct lockup for "protective custody." He was initially described by the arresting officer as being heavily intoxicated, agitated, and crying. During the first few hours of incarceration, the booking officer periodically observed the decedent as having "glassy eyes...in a stupor" with behavior ranging from confusion to hysteria. The booking officer subsequently discovered the decedent hanging from the cell bars by his trousers. He was cut down and paramedics were called, but the booking officer did not initiate any life-saving measures. The plaintiff filed suit alleging that the city violated the decedent's constitutional right to due process "through a policy or custom of inattention amounting to deliberate indifference to the serious medical needs of intoxicated and potentially suicidal detainees." At trial, the plaintiff offered evidence which showed that from 1980 through 1985, the city's police department experienced 20 suicides in its lockups, did not provide suicide prevention training to its officers nor intake screening for suicide risk to its inmates, or any other suicide prevention measures.

In affirming the jury verdict, the appeals court stated that "the evidence of 20 jail suicides in the Philadelphia prison system between 1980-85, of whom 15 were intoxicated, *the City's possession of knowledge before 1981 that intoxicated detainees presented a high risk of suicide, its awareness of published standards for suicide prevention, and its failure to implement recommendations of experts, including its own director of mental health services for the prison system, was sufficient basis for the jury to have found the unnamed officials with responsibility over the City's prisons acted recklessly or with deliberate indifference, thereby contributing to the deprivation of constitutional rights of plaintiff's* decedent *If a city cannot be held liable when its policy makers had notice of a problem and failed to act, then it is difficult to posit a set of facts on which a city could be held liable to have been deliberately indifferent."* The ruling also affirmed the lower court award of over $1.1 million in wrongful death, survival damages, and delayed damages to the plaintiff.

5) ***Cunningham v. Tkadletz*** [97 C 1109, Federal District Court for the Northern District of Illinois, 1998]
Natiera Cunningham, 18-years-old, was arrested for misdemeanor offenses arising out of an alleged shoplifting incident. She was subsequently transferred to, and incarcerated in, the Gurnee, Illinois police lockup. Natiera was held on the misdemeanor charges, as well as on an outstanding felony warrant from Waukegan, Illinois. Shortly before midnight the same day she was arrested, Natiera attempted to commit suicide in the Gurnee lockup by preparing to hang herself with an article of clothing. Gurnee police, who maintained video surveillance of prisoners in their lockup, observed her and immediately intervened, preventing the suicide. Natiera was transported to a nearby hospital, briefly examined, and returned to the custody of the Gurnee police. Hospital discharge instructions directed that Natiera be placed on a "suicide watch," which was maintained by the Gurnee police for the duration of the night.

Waukegan Police Department Detective Mark Tkadletz spoke by telephone with a Gurnee police commander the next morning. After being apprized of Natiera's suicide attempt some 9 hours earlier, he drove to Gurnee to take custody of Cunningham for the purpose of interrogating her regarding the outstanding felony charge. Two Gurnee police commanders later testified at trial that Detective Tkadletz was informed in detail of Natiera's earlier attempted suicide and was apprized that her mother was concerned that she would attempt suicide again. The commanders advised Detective Tkadletz that they considered Natiera to be at continued risk of attempting to commit suicide.

Detective Tkadletz took custody of Natiera and transported her to the Waukegan Police Department. While at the police station, he interrogated the young woman regarding the pending felony charge for approximately 30 minutes during which, by his own report, she became increasingly upset, and ultimately stopped answering his questions. Detective Tkadletz subsequently took Natiera to court for a bond hearing. He never relayed any of the information he received concerning Natiera's suicide attempt or her continuing risk of suicide to court deputies, or to anyone else.

Natiera was remanded to the Lake County Jail in Waukegan. Laarni Dazal, a nurse for Correctional Medical Services (CMS), a private contractor providing medical and mental health services at the facility, administered a suicide risk screening form on Natiera. The form consisted of a series of questions and observations. The answers given were recorded on a form and tallied to provide a numerical score. CMS regulations provided that a score of eight or higher required an immediate psychiatric referral. Although Natiera scored an "eight" on the form, Nurse Dazal failed to make a psychiatric referral or otherwise notify the jail authorities that the inmate might be suicidal. In a subsequent affidavit, the nurse stated she failed to make a psychiatric referral because she did not believe the truthfulness of some of Natiera's answers, i.e., her score was not a "legitimate eight." Accordingly, Natiera was not afforded any psychiatric treatment and was placed in the general jail population, without benefit of any type of suicide watch, or other precautions.

During her confinement, Natiera became increasingly frustrated and agitated over the inability of her family to raise money to bond her out of jail. For the next two days, she made repeated calls home, to no avail. At approximately 9:00 am on the morning of June 6, Natiera was told she was not scheduled to go to court or to be released that day. She became "disruptive" and was placed on 23-hour lock down by Erica Sandahl, a Lake County correctional officer working on the housing tier to which Natiera was assigned. Officer Sandahl returned to the housing tier from lunch at approximately 12:15 pm. Former inmates who testified at trial stated that Natiera had refused to eat her lunch that day, and had been pleading from her cell for someone to speak to. Other plaintiff witnesses testified that, while Natiera was calling out for help, Officer Sandahl remained in the day room watching a soap opera with inmates who were not on lock down. There was, however, no testimony offered at trial to suggest that Officer Sandahl had been told anything about Natiera having attempted suicide or expressing any desire to harm herself. At the end of the television program, the officer went to Natiera's cell and found her hanging from an overhead sprinkler. Emergency medical assistance was called. Shortly thereafter, Natiera Cunningham was pronounced dead at a nearby hospital.

In his trial testimony, Detective Tkadletz admitted he was informed of Natiera's earlier suicide attempt, but adamantly denied he was told that there was any continuing concern that the young woman remained at risk of suicide. The detective further maintained that since Natiera had been "treated and released" at a hospital, he was fully justified in concluding there was no reason to believe that she was at continued risk of committing suicide. He maintained, therefore, there was no need for him to have informed the sheriff's deputies of Natiera's suicide attempt the previous night. Detective Tkadletz also maintained that Natiera did not "appear suicidal" or "depressed," and testified that her demeanor was similar to that of other arrestees with pending felony charges.

*A settlement of all claims against Correctional Medical Services and Nurse Dazal was arrived at in advance of trial. The claim against Officer Sandahl was dismissed by the trial judge at the conclusion of the plaintiff's evidence. On October 28, 1998, an eight-person jury returned a verdict in favor of the plaintiffs and against Detective Tkadletz, totaling $1,350,000, including $750,000 in punitive damages.*

6) *Jacobs v. West Feliciana Sheriff's Department* [WL 1289478, 5th Cir., 2000]. On August 21, 1996, Sheila Jacobs was arrested for the attempted, second-degree murder, by shooting, of her uncle. Jacobs had become enraged at her uncle when she learned that he had allegedly sexually molested one of her sons years before. The arresting state troopers informed an investigator for the West Feliciana Sheriff's Department that Jacobs told them shortly after her arrest that, after shooting her uncle, she had tried to kill herself by placing a loaded gun in her mouth and pulling the trigger, but the gun had jammed. The investigator conveyed this information to Sheriff Bill Daniel and Deputies Earl Reech and Wayne Rabalais.

After processing Jacobs, the officers at the West Feliciana Parish Prison placed Jacobs in a "detox" cell. According to Deputy Rabalais, when Jacobs was placed in the detox cell, the officers had her on suicide watch and had placed a note to that effect in the control center. Although a portion of the detox cell could be observed from the jail's control room through a window, a substantial amount of the cell (including the bunk area) fell into a "blind spot" and was not visible from the control room. This cell could be completely observed only if an officer viewed it from the hallway. The cell also had several "tie-off" points (bars and light fixtures from which a makeshift rope could be suspended), despite Sheriff Daniel's acknowledgment that a suicide prevention cell should not have such tie off points and despite the fact that another inmate (James Halley) had previously committed suicide in the very same cell by hanging himself with a sheet from one of these tie-off points. To the best of Deputy Rabalais's knowledge, and pursuant to Sheriff Daniel's directive, Jacobs was not given sheets on the first night of her detention, August 21.

On the morning of August 23, an attorney visited Jacobs at the jail. He requested that Sheriff Daniel leave Jacobs in the detox cell, and perhaps provide her with a blanket and towel. Sheriff Daniel instructed one of his deputies to give these items to Jacobs, but the record reflects only that Jacobs received a sheet (which she eventually used to kill herself), and there is no evidence that she received either a towel or a blanket.

Deputies Earl Reech and Rabalais were on duty at the West Feliciana jail facility from 11:30 p.m. the night of August 23, until 7:30 a.m. the next morning, August 24, 1996. The record reveals that the defendants still regarded Jacobs as a suicide risk during that time. Indeed, Sheriff Daniel testified that Jacobs was on a "precautionary," though not a "straight" suicide watch. Our review of the record reveals few discernible differences between these two types of suicide watches. When an inmate was on "strict" suicide watch, the informal policy at the jail was to have the inmate checked on every fifteen minutes. Deputy Reech testified that he and Deputy Rabalais made periodic checks on Jacobs; however, it is unclear exactly how often the deputies checked on Jacobs while she was under the "precautionary" suicide watch. What is clear is that as many as 45 minutes elapsed from the time a deputy last checked on Jacobs to the time she was discovered hanging from the light fixture in the detox cell.

Specifically, the record reveals that, after having observed Jacobs in the detox cell at 12:22 a.m. and 1:00 a.m., Deputy Reech checked on Jacobs at 1:22 a.m., and he observed her lying awake in her bunk. At 2:00 a.m., Deputy Rabalais went to investigate some loud music down the hall, and on his way back to the control station, he observed Jacobs lying awake in her bunk. Deputy Rabalais testified that both he and Deputy Reech checked on Jacobs sometime between 2:00 and 2:44 a.m., and that Jacobs was still awake in her bunk. After this last check, Deputy Reech returned to the jail lobby to read his newspaper. At approximately 2:44 a.m., Deputy Rabalais looked into the detox cell from the control room and saw what appeared to be part of an arm hanging from the ceiling. Concerned, he went to find Deputy Reech, who was still reading the newspaper, to help him get into the detox cell. When the deputies arrived at the cell, they found Jacobs hanging from a sheet that had been tied around the caging surrounding a ceiling light fixture. Deputy Rabalais found a knife and enlisted the assistance of another inmate in cutting the sheet and lowering Jacobs onto the floor. By all indications, Jacobs had torn a small string from the bunk mattress and wrapped that string around the sheet to form a make-shift rope. The paramedics who arrived only moments later were unable to resuscitate Jacobs. Jacobs's suicide was the third suicide at the jail during Sheriff Daniel's tenure there. As noted above, James Halley's suicide had occurred in the same cell where Jacobs killed herself. The third suicide had occurred in a cell down the hallway from the detox cell. The family of Sheila Jacobs filed suit.

On September 13, 2000, the United States Court of Appeals for the 5th Circuit ruled that the family had sufficient grounds to sue then-Sheriff Bill Daniel and Deputy Rabalais. The court stated, in part, that:

"The record before us reveals that Sheriff Daniel was aware that Jacobs had tried to kill herself once before and that she posed a serious risk of trying to do so again. Throughout the time Jacobs was in the jail, Sheriff Daniel considered her to be a suicide risk. Under Sheriff Daniel's supervision, Jacobs was placed in the detox cell, which had a significant blind spot and tie-off points, despite the fact that during Sheriff Daniel's tenure another detainee, James Halley, had committed suicide in the same cell by hanging himself from one of the tie-off points....Moreover, Sheriff Daniel ordered his deputies to give Jacobs a blanket and towel, despite the fact that he still knew that she was a suicide risk. He did not offer any reason for doing so other than Jacobs's appointed counsel's suggestion that she be given these items, and in fact, he acknowledged that a suicidal person should not have loose bedding of any kind in a cell with them. Sheriff Daniel also acknowledged that it was not advisable to place a suicidal detainee in a cell with tie-off points, even though the detox cell had tie-off points. We note also that with full awareness that a prior suicide occurred in the detox cell by way of an inmate securing a blanket to a tie-off point therein, Sheriff Daniel did nothing to eliminate or conceal the tie off points in the detox cell, which cell Sheriff Daniel's own unwritten policy mandated as the appropriate cell for housing suicidal detainees....*We would find it difficult to say that this behavior could not support a jury finding that Sheriff Daniels acted with deliberate indifference, and likewise we find it even more difficult to say that this conduct was objectively reasonable.* For these reasons, as well as for substantially the same as those reasons given in the Magistrate Judge's order denying summary judgment, we affirm the denial of qualified immunity for Sheriff Daniel as to claims asserted against him in his individual capacity....

....Deputy Reech was the senior deputy on duty when Jacobs killed herself. Like Sheriff Daniel and Deputy Rabalais, he had actual knowledge that Jacobs was a suicide risk at all times during her detention. He also knew about the earlier hanging suicide of James Halley in the detox room, and with respect to the Halley and Jacobs suicides, Reech deposed that there was nothing they (at the jail) could do to stop the detainees from killing themselves if they wanted to and that it wasn't their responsibility. Despite this knowledge, and the fact that nothing had been done to correct either the blind spot or the tie-off points in the detox cell, Deputy Reech ordered Jacobs to be placed in it for a suicide watch. Like Sheriff Daniel, Deputy Reech was on notice that these facilities were 'obviously inadequate'....

....We note that it was Sheriff Daniel, not Deputy Reech, who made the decision that Jacobs be given a blanket. The fact that Reech did not make the decision that Jacobs should have a blanket would seem to militate in favor of finding qualified immunity, since after all, if no blanket had ever been provided, it would not have made any difference which cell he had placed her in. On the other hand, Deputy Reech did observe Jacobs lying on the bunk in the detox cell several times during the period when she had the sheet, and despite his awareness that a prior suicide occurred in the detox cell using a blanket and that suicidal inmates should not be given lose bedding, he did not take the sheet away from Jacobs. Additionally, Deputy Reech did not check on Jacobs as frequently as he was supposed to....

....Given Deputy Reech's level of knowledge about the significant risk that Jacobs would attempt to harm herself and his disregard for precautions he knew should be taken, we conclude that there is enough evidence in this record from which a reasonable jury could find subjective deliberate indifference. And in light of Deputy Reech's failure to insure that adequate precautions were taken to protect Jacobs from her known suicidal tendencies, we find that Deputy Reech's conduct falls outside the realm of that which could be characterized as being objectively reasonable in light of the duty to not act with subjective deliberate indifference to a known substantial risk of suicide....

....We conclude that no reasonable jury could find that Deputy Rabalais, who had only been on the job for about six months at the time of Jacob's death, acted with deliberate indifference, and we further find that his conduct, in light of the record evidence, was objectively reasonable, thus entitling him to qualified immunity from suit in his individual capacity. While Deputy Rabalais, like his co-defendants, had actual knowledge that Jacobs was a suicide risk at all times during her confinement, he did not make the decision to place her in the detox cell. As noted above, Deputy Reech, the senior deputy on duty with over twenty years of experience, made that decision. Deputy Rabalais likewise had nothing to do with the order that Jacobs be given a blanket and towel, which order was evidently interpreted by some unknown jail official as entitling Jacobs to a loose sheet instead....

....The only element of Jacobs's detention over which Deputy Rabalais had direct control was the frequency with which he checked on her. Like Deputy Reech, Deputy Rabalais did not comply with Sheriff Daniel's unwritten policy of checking on Jacobs every fifteen minutes. However, this failure to abide by Sheriff Daniel's policy alone evinces at best, negligence on the part of Deputy Rabalais, which is insufficient to support a finding of deliberate indifference....

....As a result of the foregoing analysis, we dismiss this appeal as it relates to the official capacity claims asserted against Sheriff Daniel for a lack of interlocutory appellate jurisdiction, we affirm in part the Magistrate Judge's order to the extent that it denies summary judgment on grounds of qualified immunity on the individual capacity claims asserted against Sheriff Daniel and Deputy Reech, and we reverse in part the Magistrate Judge's order to the extent it denies summary judgment on grounds of qualified immunity on the individual capacity claims asserted against Deputy Rabalais and we remand to the district court for entry of judgment in his favor."

**ATTACHMENT 4**

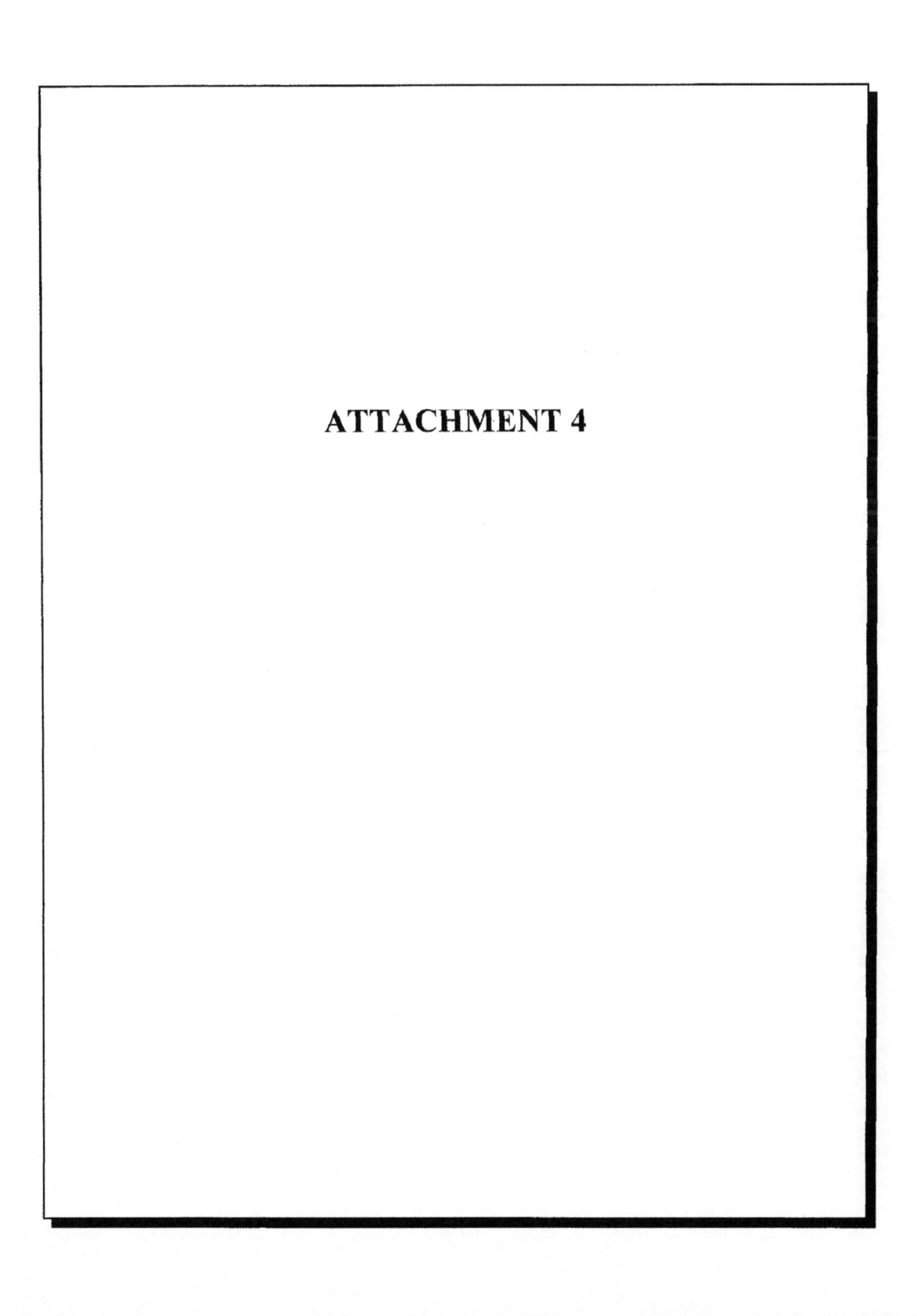

# THE MORTALITY REVIEW

*This is a suggested format for conducting a mortality review.*

## TRAINING

- Had all correctional, medical, and mental health staff involved in the incident previously received training in the area of suicide prevention?

- Had all staff who responded to the incident previously received training (and are currently certified) in standard first aid and cardiopulmonary resuscitation (CPR)?

## IDENTIFICATION/SCREENING

- Had the inmate been properly screened for potentially suicidal behavior upon entry into the facility?

- Did the screening include inquiry regarding: past suicidal ideation and/or attempts; significant loss (job, relationship, death of family member/close friend, etc.); history of suicidal behavior by family member/close friend; suicide risk during prior confinement; if arresting/transporting officer believes inmate is currently at risk?

- If the screening process indicated a potential risk for suicide, was the inmate properly referred to mental health and/or medical personnel?

## COMMUNICATION

- Was there information regarding the inmate's prior and/or current suicide risk from outside agencies that was not communicated to the correctional facility?

- Was there information regarding the inmate's prior and/or current suicide risk from throughout the facility to appropriate personnel?

- Did the inmate engage in any type of behavior that might have been indicative of a potential risk of suicide? If so, was this observed behavior communicated throughout the facility to appropriate personnel?

## HOUSING

- Where was the inmate housed and why was he or she assigned to this housing unit?

- Was there anything regarding the physical design of the inmate's cell and or/housing unit that contributed to the suicide (e.g., poor visibility, protrusions in cell conducive to hanging attempts, etc.)?

## LEVELS OF SUPERVISION

- What level and frequency of supervision was the inmate under immediately prior to the incident?

- Given the inmate's observed behavior prior to the incident, was the level of supervision adequate?

- When was the inmate last physically observed by staff prior to the incident?

- If the inmate was not physically observed within the required time interval prior to the incident, what reason(s) was determined to cause the delay in supervision?

- Was the inmate on a mental health caseload? If so, what was the frequency of contact between the inmate and mental health personnel? When was the inmate last seen by mental health personnel?

- If the inmate was not on a mental health caseload, should he or she have been?

- If the inmate was not on suicide watch at the time of the incident, should he or she have been?

## INTERVENTION

- Did the staff member(s) who discovered the inmate follow proper intervention procedures such as: survey the scene to ensure the emergency was genuine; call for back-up support; ensure that medical personnel were immediately notified; and begin standard first aid and/or CPR?

- Did the inmate's housing unit contain proper emergency equipment for correctional staff to effectively respond to a suicide attempt, i.e., first aid kit, pocket mask or mouth shield, Ambu bag, and rescue tool (to quickly cut through fibrous material)?

- Were there any delays in either correctional or medical personnel responding immediately to the incident?

- Were medical personnel properly notified as to the nature of the emergency and did they respond with appropriate equipment?

- Was all the medical equipment working properly?

## REPORTING

- Were all appropriate officials and personnel notified of the incident in a timely manner?

- Were other notifications, including the inmate's family and appropriate outside authorities, made in a timely manner?

- Did all staff who came into contact with the inmate prior to the incident submit a report and/or statement as to their full knowledge of the inmate and incident? Was there any reason to question the accuracy and/or completeness of any report and/or statement?

## FOLLOW-UP

- Were all affected staff and inmates offered critical incident stress debriefing following the incident?

- Were there any other investigations conducted (or that should be authorized) into the incident that may be helpful to the mortality review?

- Were there any findings and/or recommendations from previous mortality reviews of inmate suicides that were relevant to this mortality review?

- As a result of this mortality review, what recommendations (if any) are necessary for revision in policy, training, physical plan, medical or mental health services, and operation procedures to reduce the likelihood of future incidents.

*Developed by Lindsay M. Hayes*

On May 1, 1996, the inmate's mother contacted a jail official and demanded an explanation as to why her daughter had not received her Zoloft medication. The jail official promised to look into the matter and instructed Susan Sussman, the jail's health services coordinator to investigate the allegation. Ms. Sussman reviewed the medical chart, found no explanation, and talked with Dr. Harvey Loth, the jail psychiatrist. She was told by Dr. Loth that Nancy Bloom did not want Zoloft because it made her violent. Ms. Sussman instructed Dr. Loth to document this information in the medical chart. There was other subsequent information made available, however, to suggest that Dr. Loth simply made a decision that Ms. Bloom did not need Zoloft or any other psychotropic medication, and that the psychiatrist had not reviewed the inmate's case file which indicated a significant mental health history.

At approximately 5:00 pm on May 5, 1996, an inmate in B-Block approached Officer Marie Deerfield and stated that Nancy Bloom had told her that "if she didn't get bailed out she was gonna kill herself." (Aside from this statement, there were *no* other indications that jail staff were aware of any current suicidal behavior or statements by Ms. Bloom during her 30-day incarceration in the West County Jail.) Officer Deerfield immediately called Captain Linda Hoffman who ordered that Ms. Bloom be assigned an inmate aide "1:1" until seen by either medical or mental health staff. Ms. Bloom was seen by Nurse Ronald Saunders at 6:15 pm. Following his assessment, Nurse Saunders felt that close watch status was not necessary and Ms. Bloom was returned to B-Block with a recommendation for "general population." Despite this recommendation, Officer Deerfield remained concerned about Ms. Bloom and recommended to Captain Hoffman that the inmate be maintained on "1:1" with an inmate aide until she could be assessed by Dr. Boseman the following day. Captain Hoffman then ordered the continuation of the "1:1" status. Dr. Boseman assessed Ms. Bloom on the morning of May 6 and terminated the close watch status.

At approximately 4:30 pm on May 16, 1996, Nancy Bloom was talking with her mother on the telephone when she began experiencing a nose bleed. Jail staff immediately referred her to medical staff for treatment. Jail staff noticed that she seemed upset and crying, apparently concerned about the severity of the nose blood. According to her mother, however, she believed Nancy was potentially suicidal and upset about the prospect of being sent to prison. She later called the jail and spoke with Sergeant Thomas Flower. According to Sergeant Flower's "special report" of the telephone call, Mrs. Bloom was concerned about her daughter's medical condition, not only the nose bleed but, in light of a "history of suicidal tendencies," her being upset about the prospect of going to prison. Sergeant Flower told Mrs. Bloom that medical staff had treated the nose bleed, that he would make sure that mental health staff were made aware of her concerns, and he would assign an inmate aide to watch her daughter.

According to Sergeant Flower, he also left a note in Dr. Boseman's mail box for Nancy Bloom to be seen the following morning and (according to his special report) "as a precautionary measure I instructed c/o Cullen to hire an extra aide due to inmate's condition and information received." There is no indication that use of the inmate aide to observe Nancy Bloom was extended into the next shift and, according to Dr. Boseman, she never received a note from Sergeant Flower.

During the early evening of May 16, Nancy Bloom talked with her therapist in the community, Dr. Christine Daigle, by telephone. Dr. Daigle found Ms. Bloom to be very agitated, but not overtly sad or depressed, or threatening to harm herself. In fact, they agreed that Dr. Daigle would visit the jail the following Tuesday (May 21). According to Dr. Daigle: "She was not - she was not overtly sad or depressed at that point. She was more - manic is too strong a word. But, she was excitable and kind of unrealistic in her tone and in her mood. She talked about escaping. That she and Louie (her boyfriend who was also in the jail) would escape. That she wasn't going to stay in jail ....I was not worried about her imminent death."

At approximately 11:00 pm on May 17, 1996, Nancy Bloom was found hanging from a bed sheet tied to the window knob in her cell during a routine cell check by jail staff. She had last been seen alive approximately 30 minutes earlier. CPR was initiated by jail staff, medical staff arrived within a few minutes, and Nancy Bloom was later transported to the hospital where she subsequently died.

## QUESTIONS:

### 1) WERE ANY JAIL, MEDICAL, AND/OR MENTAL HEALTH STAFF (OR AGENCY OFFICIALS) <u>NEGLIGENT</u>?

### 2) WERE ANY JAIL, MEDICAL, AND/OR MENTAL HEALTH STAFF (OR AGENCY OFFICIALS) <u>DELIBERATELY INDIFFERENT</u>?

# Suicide Prevention: Aftermath of a Suicide
(June 27, 2001, 3:15-4:45pm)

# REPORTING

o In the event of a suicide attempt or suicide, all appropriate officials should be notified through the chain of command.

o Following the incident, the victim's family should be immediately notified, as well as appropriate outside authorities.

o All staff who came into contact with the victim prior to the incident should be required to submit a statement that includes their full knowledge of the inmate and incident. Their reports should be brief, accurate, and specific to personal knowledge of the incident -- and not what they assumed or thought happened.

o **NEVER PLAY CATCH-UP WITH THE LOGS**

# CRITICAL INCIDENT STRESS DEBRIEFING

"**Critical incident debriefing**. Responding to and/or observing a suicide in progress can be extremely stressful for staff and inmates. The plan should specify the procedures for offering critical incident debriefing to all affected personnel and inmates." (NCCHC, 1997)

o Debriefing must be legitimate, not simply a paper policy, administration must show employees that it cares about their future and willing to support the CISD process.

o Debriefing can be either formal or informal, must be offered on a voluntary basis.

o Debriefing must be strictly confidential, <u>not</u> be associated with investigative or administrative review of inmate's suicide, or issues of potential liability.

o Debriefing can be offered through corrections department, employee assistance program, local mental health provider, or community CISD Team.

o Debriefing should be held with 24 to 72 hours of incident.

o Debriefings, normally 2 to 4 hours in length, provide affected staff with opportunity to process their thoughts and feelings about the incident, create an understanding of critical stress symptoms, and develop ways of dealing with those symptoms.

o When appropriate, staff should be encouraged to seek further assistance beyond the CISD process.

# MORTALITY REVIEW

Every completed suicide, as well as suicide attempt that requires hospitalization, should be examined by a mortality review. The purpose of a mortality review is straightforward:

> *What happened in the case under review and what can be learned to reduce the likelihood of future incidents.*

The mortality review team must be multidisciplinary and include direct care, mental health and medical personnel. Exclusion of one or more disciplines will severely jeopardize the integrity of the mortality review.

The mortality review, separate and apart from other formal investigations that may be required to determine the cause of death, should include:

1) critical review of the circumstances surrounding the incident;

2) critical review of facility procedures relevant to the incident;

3) synopsis of all relevant training received by involved staff;

4) pertinent medical and mental health services/reports involving the victim; and

5) recommendations, if any, for change in policy, training, physical plant, medical or mental health services, and operational procedures.

# MORTALITY REVIEW OF INMATE SUICIDES AND THE CASE OF GEORGE MOFFAT[2]

## THE CASE

On the evening of May 17, 1997, George Moffat (a pseudonym) was arrested for domestic violence against his wife Sheila and transported to a county jail in a midwestern state. During transport, he tried to cut his wrists while handcuffed in the back of the patrol car. Although the wounds appeared superficial, Mr. Moffat was transported to the local hospital for medical treatment. "It's a common thing. People cut their wrists thinking it will keep them out of jail. It doesn't work," commented Matthew Stevens, the arresting and transporting officer.

Upon arrival at the county jail, Mr. Moffat was booked and processed without incident, although jail staff determined that he was currently on probation for burglary. Nurse Laura Thompson completed a medical intake screening form. The 54-year-old inmate listed several problems, including gout, high blood pressure and back pain. Mr. Moffat also admitted that he had attempted suicide approximately four months ago by cutting his wrists, and had spent three days in the state hospital. No mention was made of the wrist cutting in the patrol car a few hours earlier and Mr. Moffat denied any current suicidal ideation. Although Nurse Thompson did not feel that his prior suicide attempt several months earlier justified any current preventative measures, as a precautionary matter, she filled out a referral slip for further assessment the following morning by the facility's mental health staff. The referral slip was placed in the mental health services' mailbox in the receiving and discharge unit. Mr. Moffat was then classified and subsequently placed in a general population housing unit.

George Moffat remained in the county jail for approximately six months. During this time, he received medical treatment when requested for his gout, high blood pressure, and back pain. He never requested mental health services, nor was he ever assessed by clinicians as a result of Nurse Thompson's initial referral. Mr. Moffat appeared in court several times, eventually pleading guilty to the domestic violence charge and receiving a county jail sentence. A separate hearing on whether to revoke his probation, which in all likelihood would result in a state prison sentence, was scheduled for the first week of December 1997. During his six months of incarceration, Mr. Moffat had little contact with his family. His two adult daughters refused to visit him in jail and his wife had contacted an attorney with the intent of filing for divorce.

---

[2]In order to ensure complete confidentiality, the names of the victim, facility, and staff have been changed. No other modifications to the facts of this case have been made.

On Saturday, November 22, 1997, Mr. Moffat called his wife over a dozen times and threatened to kill himself if she filed for divorce. He also appeared distraught at the prospect of going to prison. During one telephone call, Mr. Moffat told his wife that he was tearing his bed sheet into strips. Because she had heard her husband threaten suicide in the past and, in fact, he had attempted suicide at the same facility the previous year, Sheila Moffat was concerned about her husband's state of mind and called the county jail. She spoke with Lieutenant Skip Morrow who gave assurances that her husband would be safe. Following the telephone conversation, Lieutenant Morrow went to Mr. Moffat's housing unit and instructed Officer Daniel Anders to check the inmate's cell. When Officer Anders approached the cell he noticed that a strip of bed sheet was tied to the cell bars. Mr. Moffat was sitting on his bunk and appeared nervous. When the officer inquired as to why the cloth was tied to the bars, Mr. Moffat offered no explanation other than to deny that he was contemplating suicide. Officer Anders removed the cloth from the bars, confiscated the remainder of the bed sheet, and reported back to Lieutenant Morrow. The officer was instructed to write a report of the incident (to include the fact that Mr. Moffat had denied being suicidal) and forward a copy to mental health staff.

During the next several hours, Officer Anders checked Mr. Moffat's cell on an hourly basis. The inmate appeared to be sleeping during a cell check at 11:10 pm. However, during a cell check at approximately 12:07 am on November 23, the officer observed George Moffat sitting on the floor with his back to the cell door. The leg of his jumpsuit was tied around his neck and through the cell bars. Officer Anders ran back to the control booth in the housing unit, instructed an officer to call for back-up support and medical personnel, grabbed a pair of medical shears from the first aid kit, and returned to the cell. The officer used the shears to cut the cloth away from the bars. Mr. Moffat's body fell to the floor. Other correctional staff arrived, the cell door was opened, and the inmate was pulled out into the hallway. An officer checked for vital signs and found none. Although trained in cardiopulmonary resuscitation (CPR), the officers did not initiate CPR, rather they waited for medical staff to arrive. A jail nurse arrived several minutes later and initiated CPR, assisted by a correctional officer who used a mouth shield from a pouch attached to his belt. Emergency Medical Services personnel arrived at 12:16 am and continued CPR. Mr. Moffat was subsequently transported to the hospital and pronounced dead upon arrival. Following his death, timely notification was made to both designated facility officials and Mr. Moffat's family.

Several investigations were conducted into the suicide of George Moffat. The first inquiry was the medical autopsy in which a forensic pathologist concluded that the cause of death was "asphyxia due to hanging." Next, the state police conducted an inquiry. A state trooper interviewed several correctional staff, reviewed incident reports from all involved staff, and inspected the cell area. His investigation lasted almost a full day and a subsequent two-page report concluded that the death was a suicide with no signs of foul play.

As per departmentral policy, the county jail's mental health services administrator also reviewed Mr. Moffat's suicide. The inquiry was limited to a review of the inmate's medical file, and did not include any staff interviews. The mental health administrator summarized her document review of George Moffat's suicide in a one-paragraph confidential report self-titled a "psychological autopsy." The report is reprinted in its entirety as follows:

> The inmate, George Moffat, was admitted to the county jail on May 17, 1997. This inmate had written several medical requests, all of which were related to such discomforts as foot problems, colds, lower back pain, and rashes. He never requested mental health assistance, therefore Mental Health Services never had an opportunity to interview, evaluate or treat him throughout the six months of his incarceration. Based upon a review of the medical file, there is no evidence that this inmate's death could have been prevented.

The mental health administrator, however, did conduct a one-hour suicide prevention workshop for correctional staff several months after Mr. Moffat's death, the first such training for any departmental personnel in over 10 years.

George Moffat's suicide was also reviewed by the county prosecutor's office. An investigator from that office reviewed both Mr. Moffat's institutional and medical file, state police report, autopsy report, and transcription of the coroner's inquest. Based upon this review, the county prosecutor wrote a letter to the county sheriff which stated, in part, that "we limited the scope of our investigation to reviewing whether or not George Moffat died as a result of an unlawful homicide or suicide. It is clear that he died from his own actions. It is impossible to determine whether or not this inmate intended to take his own life. He may well have died accidentally while feigning suicide. Quite frankly, that was not really our concern. He clearly died by his own actions. We consider this case closed."

Shortly after receiving the county prosecutor's letter, Sheriff Roy Hamilton issued a press release on April 27, 1998 stating that George Moffat's suicide had been investigated thoroughly by several agencies and each concluded that there was no criminal wrongdoing by any county jail personnel. When asked by a local newspaper reporter the following day whether he planned to make any changes in the 850-bed jail in light of Mr. Moffat's death, as well as two other inmate suicides during 1997, Sheriff Hamilton responded that "as far as we are concerned, this matter is over. There was no criminal involvement here. My concern is more if we suspect foul play. I have no idea why these inmates commit suicide in my jail. If I did, I could probably do a better job of preventing it."

## THE MORTALITY REVIEW

*The purpose of a mortality review of an inmate suicide is straightforward: What happened in the case under review and what can be learned to reduce the likelihood of future incidents. The mortality review team must be multidisciplinary and include correctional, mental health and medical personnel. Exclusion of one or more disciplines will severely jeopardize the integrity of the mortality review. Detailed below is a suggested format and areas of inquiry for conducting a mortality review.*

1) **Training**

   o Had all correctional, medical, and mental health staff involved in the incident previously received training in the area of suicide prevention?

   o Had all staff who responded to the incident previously received training (and are currently certified) in standard first aid and cardiopulmonary resuscitation (CPR)?

2) **Identification/Screening**

   o Had the inmate been properly screened for potentially suicidal behavior upon entry into the facility?

   o Did the screening include inquiry regarding: past suicidal ideation and/or attempts; current ideation, threat, plan; prior mental health treatment/hospitalization; recent significant loss (job, relationship, death of family member/close friend, etc.); history of suicidal behavior by family member/close friend; suicide risk during prior confinement; arresting/transporting officer(s) believes inmate is currently at risk?

   o If the screening process indicated a potential risk for suicide, was the inmate properly referred to mental health and/or medical personnel?

3) **Communication**

   o Was there information regarding the inmate's prior and/or current suicide risk from outside agencies that was not communicated to the correctional facility?

   o Was there information regarding the inmate's prior and/or current suicide risk from correctional, mental health and/or medical personnel that was not communicated throughout the facility to appropriate personnel?

   o Did the inmate engage in any type of behavior that might have been indicative of a potential risk of suicide? If so, was this observed behavior communicated throughout the facility to appropriate personnel?

4) **Housing**

   o Where was the inmate housed and why was he/she assigned to this housing unit?

   o Was there anything regarding the physical design of the inmate's cell and/or housing unit that contributed to the suicide (e.g., poor visibility, protrusions in cell conducive to hanging attempts, etc.)?

5) **Levels of Supervision**

   o What level and frequency of supervision was the inmate under immediate prior to the incident?

   o Given the inmate's observed behavior prior to the incident, was the level of supervision adequate?

   o When was the inmate last physically observed by staff prior to the incident?

   o If the inmate was not physically observed within the required time interval prior to the incident, what reason(s) was determined to cause the delay in supervision?

   o Was the inmate on a mental health caseload? If so, what was the frequency of contact between the inmate and mental health and personnel? When was the inmate last seen by mental health personnel?

   o If the inmate was not on a mental health caseload, should he/she have been?

   o If the inmate was not on suicide watch at the time of the incident, should he/she have been?

6) **Intervention**

   o Did the staff member(s) who discovered the inmate follow proper intervention procedures, i.e., surveyed the scene to ensure the emergency was genuine, called for back-up support, ensured that medical personnel were immediately notified, and began standard first aid and/or CPR?

   o Did the inmate's housing unit contain proper emergency equipment for correctional staff to effectively respond to a suicide attempt, i.e., first aid kit, pocket mask or mouth shield, Ambu bag, and rescue tool (to quickly cut through fibrous material)?

o Were there any delays in either correctional or medical personnel responding immediately to the incident? Were medical personnel properly notified as to the nature of the emergency and did they respond with appropriate equipment? Was all the medical equipment working properly?

7) **Reporting**

o Were all appropriate officials and personnel notified of the incident in a timely manner?

o Were other notifications, including the inmate's family and appropriate outside authorities, made in a timely manner?.

o Did all staff who came into contact with the inmate prior to the incident submit a report and/or statement as to their full knowledge of the inmate and incident? Was there any reason to question the accuracy and/or completeness of any report and/or statement?

8) **Follow-up**

o Were all affected staff and inmates offered critical incident stress debriefing following the incident?

o Were there any other investigations conducted (or that should be authorized) into the incident that may be helpful to the mortality review?

o Were there any findings and/or recommendations from previous mortality reviews of inmate suicides that were relevant to this mortality review?

o As a result of this morality review, what recommendations (if any) are necessary for revisions in policy, training, physical plant, medical or mental health services, and operational procedures to reduce the likelihood of future incidents.

Developed by Lindsay M. Hayes

**Suicide Prevention: Detailed Outline of Selected Sessions**

submitted by

Bonita M. Veysey, Ph.D.

June 10, 2001

**Day Two: 8:30-10:00 Session. "Suicide Prevention: Importance to Prison Administrators and Clinicians"**

**Subsection. "What is suicide and how frequently does it occur"**
   Definitions (B. Veysey 10-15 minutes)

I.  Definitions

   A. Suicide
"Intentional self-inflicted injury that results in death"

   1. What does this definition include
   2. What does this definition exclude

SUICIDE GRID: Level of Injury by Purpose/Goal

|  | Accidental | No Death | Death |
|---|---|---|---|
| Minor Injury |  | self-harm "parasuicidality" | suicide attempt |
| Serious Injury |  | self-harm "parasuicidality" | suicide attempt |
| Death |  | suicide* | suicide |

   B. Issues of Severity (level of injury vs. death)
   Issues of Intent (assessment, prediction, management, treatment)

   C. Prisons **Different experience than jails or lock-ups**

   D. Necessary components

   1. Will
   2. Opportunity
   3. Means

**Day Two: 10:15-12:00 Session. "Guiding Principles: A Holistic Approach to the Management of Suicide Risk in Prisons"**

**Subsection. "Organizational Backdrop"**
   (B. Veysey 30 minutes)

Principles:

   Collaboration across systems (security/mental health/medical)

　　　　　　Organizational differences (MH staff as DOC employees or contracted providers)
　　　　　　Joint planning opportunities
　　　　　　Training and cross-training
　　　　　　Information sharing
　　Continuity of care
　　　　　　Pre-intake
　　　　　　Classification
　　　　　　Housing/Crisis
　　　　　　Aftercare
　　　　　　Discharge/release planning
　　Comprehensive prevention program
　　　　　　Prevention
　　　　　　Intervention
　　　　　　Aftercare
　　Know your resources (administrative, clinical and security)
　　　　　　Physical plant
　　　　　　Staff

**Day Three: 8:00-8:30 Session. "Suicide Prevention Overview"**
**(B. Veysey 30 minutes)**

Three parts to a comprehensive plan
　　　　Prevention
　　　　Intervention
　　　　Aftercare

Prevention- general prevention for all inmates
Intervention- crisis response to a suicide attempt
Aftercare-continuing care for an inmate after an attempt

Two organizational components
　　　　Clinical
　　　　Operations

Clinical-the medical and mental health treatment response to suicide prevention, intervention
　　　and aftercare
Operations-SOP for identifying, supervising and transporting inmates at risk of suicide

Suicide prevention must be 1) comprehensive and continuous and 2) with treatment and supervision staff working together

**Day Three: 10:15-11:15 Session. "Suicide Interventions"**
**(B. Veysey 60 minutes)**

Intervention-organizational and clinical response to a suicide attempt

First response: mental health vs. special ops (security)
Who has organizational responsibility on-site? Stabilization vs. safety
De-escalation techniques
Mechanical control (blankets, cuffs/shackles, physical force, taser)
Transportation to emergency care or psych unit
What happens now:
    observation (distant/camera monitoring, constant monitoring, periodic monitoring)
    restraints (mechanical and chemical)
    clothing (nothing, paper, suicide gowns)
Principles
    facility resources (observation cells)
    take all threats seriously
    safety first
    increase response time
    reduce sources of harm
    reduce use of force

**Day Three: 1:00-3:00 Session. "Special Needs"**
**Subsection. "Female Inmates" (B. Veysey 20-30 minutes)**

Women and suicide
The need to understand self-injury
appropriate approach
flash points
restraints and seclusion

NIC Presentation
Lance Couturier, Ph.D.

## SUICIDE PREVENTION IN THE DEPARTMENT OF CORRECTIONS
June 1, 2001

I. Introductory Exercise: How many know someone (family or friend) who killed self? What were your reactions? [Audience responses recorded on flip chart.]

II. Pennsylvania Department of Corrections suicide statistics:

| | | | | |
|---|---|---|---|---|
| A. | 1989 | 8 | (3rd in nation) | 18 - 19,000 |
| B. | 1990 | 7 | | 19 - 20,000 |
| C. | 1991 | 3 | | 23,000+ |
| D. | 1992 | 4 | | 24,000+ |
| E. | 1993 | 2 | | 25,000+ |
| F. | 1994 | 6 | | 26,000+ |
| G. | 1995 | 14 | | 30,000+ |
| H. | 1996 | 10/11* | | 34,000+ |
| I. | 1997 | 8/9* | | 35,000+ |
| J. | 1998 | 11 | | 36,000+ |
| K. | 1999 | 8/9* | | 36,000+ |
| L. | 2000 | 5 | | 36,000+ |
| M. | 2001 | 2** | | 36,000+ |

*In 1996, 1997, and 1999, there were suicides in the Community Corrections Centers (CCC's)

**A fatal drug overdose is under investigation

III. Potential deleterious effects of long-term institutionalization upon residents.

   A. De-individuation – become dependent upon institution to meet all needs.
   B. Life cycle damage – miss many important life experiences
   C. Estrangement – world outside changes more rapidly than the inmate
   D. Isolation – lose contact with family and friends.
   E. Disculturation – acquire at new set of values.
   F. Sensory deprivation

IV. Means of suicide in PA prisons [Present overhead]

   A. Hanging – almost all PA DOC suicides have been hangings, with a few overdoses – stress all that is needed is pressure on the carotid artery, and brain damage occurs in 4 minutes and death in 6 minutes.

   B. Cutting – until 1998 in PA DOC we had seen no fatal cuttings – there were 2 in

1998, both were inmates with heinous homicide offenses.

C. Over-dosing on drugs and/or alcohol

D. Bizarre self-mutilations by inmates with mental illness

V. Inmate suicide risk factors in the PA Department of Corrections. Many are similar to risk factors in the community.

A. Inmates with mental illness – 14% of population, but 69% of suicides

B. Abusers of alcohol and other drugs (AOD) – however, most inmates display AOD problems.

C. Male inmates – PA DOC has only had 2 female suicides since 1992; however, women compose on 4% of the DOC population.

D. White inmates – Caucasians compose 34% of the population, but account for 54 to 89% of the suicides.

E. Elderly inmates

F. Sex offenders

G. Lifers and long term offenders

H. Parole violators

I. Inmates in Community Corrections Centers (CCC's).

J. Surprisingly, we have not encountered suicides in the youthful offenders.

VI. Staff suicide is a serious problem in the PA Department of Corrections

A. Staff members are also at risk of stress related problems – correctional staff members die earlier and display higher incidents of divorce, alcoholism, stroke, hypertension, heart attaches, and suicides than civilians in the community.

B. Suicide is a significant risk factor among Corrections Officers, being 39% higher compared to the working age population.

C. In 2000, there were 3 staff suicides in a work force of approximately 14,000.

VI. PA Department of Corrections initiatives to reduce suicides

A. Comprehensive initial and on going and "cross-training" are cornerstones of suicide prevention.

B. Rewrite suicide prevention policies and develop other formal mechanisms to force better communication and collaboration between custody and clinical staff members.

1. Write-in extensive cross-references in custody and treatment policies
2. Employ "Suicide Risk Indicators Checklist for RHU's/SMU's"
3. Mandate use of 911 Emergency tools
4. Mandate anti-suicide smocks and blankets

C. Expand continuum of mental health treatment services for inmates with mental illness – present mental health services brochure

D. Divert inmates with mental illness from placement in administrative segregation, whenever possible.

E. Disseminate suicide prevention and mental health information to inmate population.

1. Publish suicide prevention brochure, printed in English and Spanish – present brochure.

2. Produce suicide prevention videotapes, in English and Spanish, to be presented to all inmates via institution's closed circuit television networks. —Show sample film from SCI-Coal or Smithfield

F. Increase comprehensiveness of clinical reviews (psychological autopsies) following all suicides and frequency of review following serious attempts.

G. Enhance programming and services for non-mentally ill inmates, including sex offenders, substance abusers, elderly inmates, and "lifers" and long term offenders

VII. Mechanisms to provide emotional support to PA Department of Corrections staff members

A. Critical Incident Stress Management (CISM)
B. Suicide prevention training.
D. Development of benefits brochure highlighting CISM, SEAP (State Employees Compensation), and Workmen's compensation.

Selected Bibliography

Cheek, F. E. (1983, February). Correctional Officer Stress. *Corrections Today*, 14, 15, 18 24.

Cooperstein, M. A. (2001, May). Corrections Officers: The forgotten police force. *Pennsylvania Psychologist Quarterly*, 61(5), 7, 18, 19, 23.

Couturier, L.C. and Maue, F.R (2000, summer). Suicide prevention initiatives in a large, statewide Department of Corrections. Jail Suicide/Mental Health Update, 9 (4), 1-8.

Jamison, K. R. (1999). *Night falls fast: Understanding suicide.* New York: Alfred A. Knopf.

Sommer, R. (1974), Tight spaces: hard architecture and how to humanize it. Englewood Cliffs, NJ, Prentice Hall.

## SUICIDE RISK INDICATORS CHECKLIST FOR RHU/SMU

Revised (6/21/99)

'E NAME: _____  DOC #: _____

MU Officer Completing Form (print): _____ Date: _____ Time: _____

1. Escorting officer has information that inmate may be a suicidal risk.
2. Inmate is expressing suicidal thoughts/making threats to harm self.
3. Inmate shows signs of depression (crying, withdrawn, passive).
4. Inmate is acting/talking in a strange manner (hearing/seeing things that aren't there).
5. Inmate appears to be under the influence of drugs/alcohol.
6. Inmate has recent family change (e.g., death of child/spouse/parent or "Dear John letter")
7. Inmate has recent legal status change (e.g., parole violation or new detainer).
8. <u>Inmate states this is his/her first placement in RHU/SMU.</u>
9. Inmate has been assaulted (physically or sexually) by another inmate.
10. Inmate shows anger, hostility, and threats.
11. Inmate appears anxious, afraid (pacing, wringing hands).
12. Inmate displays signs of self-neglect or abuse (e.g., poor hygiene or cuts and bruises).
13. Inmate states that he/she is taking psychiatric medication.

iments: _____

uctions: The ranking CO present shall ensure that this form is completed when an inmate is brought to the RHU/SMU. Th rting officer will be asked (a) why the inmate is being brought in and (b) whether there is any information that the inmate ma elf-destructive. The inmate will be asked (a) if this is his/her first time in the RHU/SMU, (b) if he/she has any speci lems or needs of which staff should be aware, (c) if he/she is on any medication, and (d) whether he/she has any rece l status changes (e.g., parole violation or detainer). The officer will also note any special physical/behavioral characteristic , crying, poor hygiene, & cuts and bruises) or if the inmate is uncooperative.

y of items #1 through #8 are checked "Yes," the RHU/SMU officer shall immediately phone the following staff:

Between 8:00 AM and 4:30 PM, nursing and Chief Psychologist or MHC. Psychologist will immediately visit the RHU/SMU review the checklist, assess the inmate, and discuss the case with RHU/SMU staff. Time of assessment will be recorded ( form.

After hours, or on weekends, the nursing staff and Shift Commander. Nurse will immediately visit RHU/SMU to revie checklist, assess the inmate, and discuss case with RHU/SMU staff. Time of assessment will be recorded on form.

At any time the inmate appears in immediate danger of harming him/herself or somebody else, the RHU/SMU staff sh also contact the Shift Commander, as well as nursing staff and Chief Psychologist or MHC to request an immedia assessment.

y of items #9 through #13 are checked, the form will be submitted to the nurse and/or psychologist the next time they visit t U/SMU, but within 24 hours. The nurse or psychologist will assess the inmate and note the date and time of assessment. T npleted form will remain in the Cumulative Adjustment Record until reviewed by PRC. Copies to Medical Record & DC-1

nical Staff Action: _____
_____ Date: _____ Time: _____
me of Clinical Staff (printed): _____ Title: _____

DC-99

# Living Through It

## Suicide Prevention

## For People in Prison

The Pennsylvania Department of Corrections gratefully acknowledges the contribution of NYS Office of Mental Health, Bureau of Forensic

---

Feeling depressed, lonely, scared, without much hope for change? For many people, perhaps like yourself, these feelings may be due to incarceration, loss of a family member, the break-up of a close relationship, or one of any number of other reasons.

Reaching out is very important at times like this and is often very difficult. When you feel low, you don't need a lecture or advice that feels like a put down. You need someone who can listen to you with respect.

*We offer you someone to talk to, someone to help you cope with your crisis!*

Here is how to get that helping hand: Contact your Unit Counselor or Unit Manager. You may also contact the psychology department by submitting a request slip. Make sure you print the following information on the slip:

NAME:      DOC #:
CELL #:      DATE:

*Feeling like you have someone to talk with gives hope!*

### How To Recognize a Crisis

People who experience a crisis may have already tried everything they can think of to solve their problem. Nothing seems to work. They may begin to feel hopeless and inadequate. This can be really scary. In fact, some people may do almost anything to escape it.

Unfortunately, many people feel that they have to solve their problems alone. Not seeing

it may be they are standing too close to the problem to see their choices. This is why trusted associate or a trained mental hea counselor can be helpful.

### Clues To Suicide

People find many ways of telling others h much they hurt. These are some of the thin you may hear:

- I can't take it any more.
- It won't matter soon.
- I'm no good anyway.
- My family would be better off witho me.

These are some of the behaviors of people wl hurt so much that they may want to atten suicide:

- Neglect of appearance or health.
- Always tired.
- Drawing away from close associates.
- Sudden edginess or restlessness.
- Talk of death or dying.
- Cutting or burning oneself.
- Collecting pills or other medications.
- Giving away prized possessions.

People who are doing any combination of the things may be experiencing emotion problems. They may be thinking of suicide.

### What You Can Do For Others:

1. Stay calm
2. Show concern.
3. Listen with respect.
4. Don't give advice that sounds like a p down.
5. Tell the CO that an inmate needs to se a counselor for help.

DC-99

# Superando El Momento

# Prevención de Suicidios en Las Cárceles

The Pennsylvania Department of Corrections gratefully acknowledges the contribution of NYS Office of Mental Health, Bureau of Forensic...

---

muchas posibilidades de mejoría? Quizás como tú, para muchas personas estos sentimientos surgen del hecho de estar encarcelados, por la muerte de algún familiar, la ruptura de una relación íntima o por un sinnúmero de otras razones.

Es importante y difícil buscar ayuda en estos momentos. Cuando te sientes sin aliento no necesitas oir un sermon o consejo que te desanime mas. Necesitas a alguien que te escuche con el respeto que tu te mereces. ¡Nosotros tenemos una persona con quien puedes hablar y que puede ayudarte a manejar tus momentos de crisis!

La siguiente es como conseguir ayuda: Habla con su consejero o director de unitario. Puede ponerse en contacto con el departmento de psicología como ponerse en el papel de cita. Es importante ponerse la sequiente información:

NOMBRE: _____ DOC Numero: _____
ELDA Numero: _____ FECHA: _____

**¡Es importante que sientas que tienes a alguien que te puede dar esperanzas!**

## Como Reconocer Una Crisis

Las personas que han experimentado una crisis pueden haber intentado resolver sus problemas de todas las formas que han creído posible. Pero nada parece funcionar. Ellos pueden empezar a sentirse desesperanzados e inadaptados. Esto los asusta. De hecho, algunas personas pueden hacer lo imposible para escapar de esto.

Desafortunadamente, muchas personas sienten que ellos tienen que resolver sus problemas solos, sin ayuda. Creyendo que nada de lo que han tratado vale la pena, pueden hacerse daño. Esto puede deberse a

---

## Indicios de Suicidio

Las personas encuentran muchas maneras de decirles a otras cuanto sufren. Estas son algunas de las cosas que usted podría escuchar:

- No aguanto más.
- Ya nada importa.
- ¡Total, si no valgo nada!
- Mis familiares estarían mejor sin mi.

Estas son algunas de las conductas que manifiestan personas, que por sentirse tan mal, desean suicidarse:

- no cuidar de su apariencia o su salud.
- sentirse siempre cansado.
- no poder dormir en las noches.
- alejarse de los compañeros mas cercanos.
- sentirse nervioso o inquieto sin motivo.
- hablar sobre temas de muerte.
- hacerse cortes o quemaduras en el cuerpo o tratar de ahorcarse.
- guardar pastillas o medicamentos con la intención de tomarlas.
- repartir o regalar objetos personales de mucho valor sentimental.

Las personas que se comportan en esta forma, generalmente experimentan problemas emocionales y pueden estar considerando el suicidio.

## Que Puedes Hacer Por Los Demás

1. Mantener la calma.
2. Mostrar interés y preocupación por lo que pasa.
3. Escucharlo con respeto.
4. No darle consejos que puedan hacerlo sentir peor.
5. Avisarle al oficial de guardia que un compañero necesita ver un consejero para que le ayude.

DC-99

# Living Through It

## Suicide Prevention

### For People in Prison

The Pennsylvania Department of Corrections gratefully acknowledges the contribution of NYS Office of Mental Health, Bureau of Forensic

---

Feeling depressed, lonely, scared, without much hope for change? For many people, perhaps like yourself, these feelings may be due to incarceration, loss of a family member, the break-up of a close relationship, or one of any number of other reasons.

Reaching out is very important at times like this and is often very difficult. When you feel low, you don't need a lecture or advice that feels like a put down. You need someone who can listen to you with respect.

*We offer you someone to talk to, someone to help you cope with your crisis!*

Here is how to get that helping hand: Contact your Unit Counselor or Unit Manager. You may also contact the psychology department by submitting a request slip. Make sure you print the following information on the slip:

NAME:      DOC #:
CELL #:      DATE:

*Feeling like you have someone to talk with gives hope!*

### How To Recognize a Crisis

People who experience a crisis may have already tried everything they can think of to solve their problem. Nothing seems to work. They may begin to feel hopeless and inadequate. This can be really scary. In fact, some people may do almost anything to escape it.

Unfortunately, many people feel that they have to solve their problems alone. Not seeing

---

it may be they are standing too close to the problem to see their choices. This is why a trusted associate or a trained mental health counselor can be helpful.

### Clues To Suicide

People find many ways of telling others how much they hurt. These are some of the things you may hear:

- I can't take it any more.
- It won't matter soon.
- I'm no good anyway.
- My family would be better off without me.

These are some of the behaviors of people who hurt so much that they may want to attempt suicide:

- Neglect of appearance or health.
- Always tired.
- Drawing away from close associates.
- Sudden edginess or restlessness.
- Talk of death or dying.
- Cutting or burning oneself.
- Collecting pills or other medications.
- Giving away prized possessions.

People who are doing any combination of these things may be experiencing emotional problems. They may be thinking of suicide.

### What You Can Do For Others:

1. Stay calm.
2. Show concern.
3. Listen with respect.
4. Don't give advice that sounds like a put down.
5. Tell the CO that an inmate needs to see a counselor for help.

DC-99

# Living Through It

## Suicide Prevention

### For People in Prison

The Pennsylvania Department of Corrections gratefully acknowledges the contribution of NYS Office of Mental Health, Bureau of Forensic

---

Feeling depressed, lonely, scared, without much hope for change? For many people, perhaps like yourself, these feelings may be due to incarceration, loss of a family member, the break-up of a close relationship, or one of any number of other reasons.

Reaching out is very important at times like this and is often very difficult. When you feel low, you don't need a lecture or advice that feels like a put down. You need someone who can listen to you with respect.

*We offer you someone to talk to, someone to help you cope with your crisis!*

Here is how to get that helping hand: Contact your Unit Counselor or Unit Manager. You may also contact the psychology department by submitting a request slip. Make sure you print the following information on the slip:

NAME:         DOC #:
CELL #:        DATE:

*Feeling like you have someone to talk with gives hope!*

## How To Recognize a Crisis

People who experience a crisis may have already tried everything they can think of to solve their problem. Nothing seems to work. They may begin to feel hopeless and inadequate. This can be really scary. In fact, some people may do almost anything to escape it.

Unfortunately, many people feel that they have to solve their problems alone. Not seeing it may be they are standing too close to the problem to see their choices. This is why a trusted associate or a trained mental health counselor can be helpful.

## Clues To Suicide

People find many ways of telling others how much they hurt. These are some of the things you may hear:

- I can't take it any more.
- It won't matter soon.
- I'm no good anyway.
- My family would be better off without me.

These are some of the behaviors of people who hurt so much that they may want to attempt suicide:

- Neglect of appearance or health.
- Always tired.
- Drawing away from close associates.
- Sudden edginess or restlessness.
- Talk of death or dying.
- Cutting or burning oneself.
- Collecting pills or other medications.
- Giving away prized possessions.

People who are doing any combination of these things may be experiencing emotional problems. They may be thinking of suicide.

### What You Can Do For Others:

1. Stay calm.
2. Show concern.
3. Listen with respect.
4. Don't give advice that sounds like a put down.
5. Tell the CO that an inmate needs to see a counselor for help.

# NIC PRISON SUICIDE PREVENTION TRAINING

Special Needs Offenders – Geriatric Inmates

Fred R. Maue, M.D.

## Trends in aging...

- Individuals age 65 and older are the fastest growing age group in America.

- Correctional systems are also experiencing the aging of their inmate populations. The number of inmates 55 and older doubled in the 9 year period from 1981 to 1990. This inmate aging trend continued in the 1990's.

- From 1985 to 1997 1/3 of the state correctional systems experienced over a 400% increase in their age 50+ inmate populations.

# In Pennsylvania...

- The number of elderly inmates grew from 206 to 832 in the thirteen year period between 1980 and 1993.
- The trend continued and during the next six years and by 12/99, the number of elderly inmates grew to 1,683 (an average of 10% per year).
- It is projected that by the end of this year our population 55 and older will reach 1,832 of the total population.

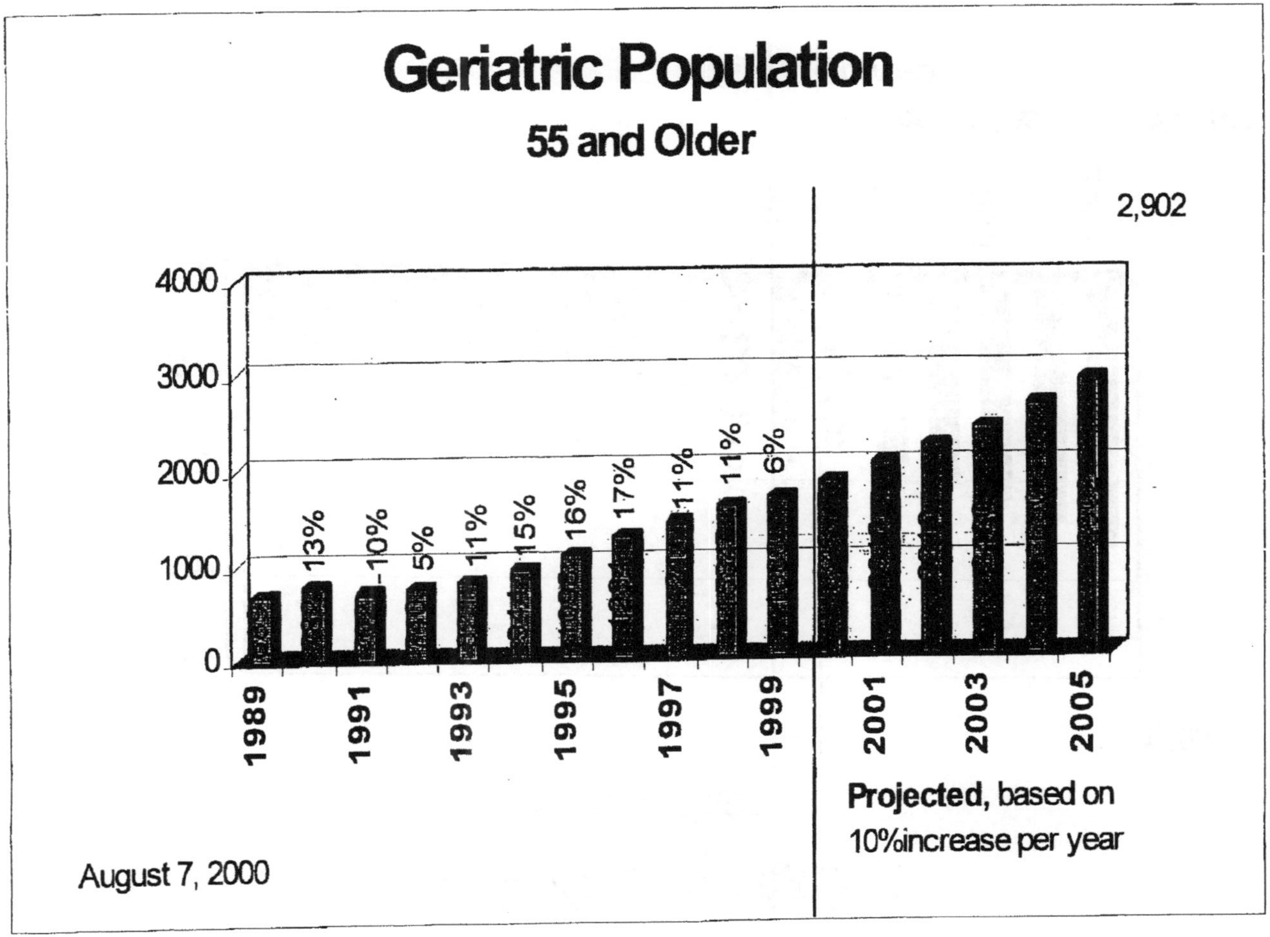

# Geriatric Population
## 55 and Older

August 7, 2000

| Year | Value | % Change |
|---|---|---|
| 1989 | | |
| 1990 | | 13% |
| 1991 | | -10% |
| 1992 | | 5% |
| 1993 | | 11% |
| 1994 | | 15% |
| 1995 | | 16% |
| 1996 | | 17% |
| 1997 | | 11% |
| 1998 | | 11% |
| 1999 | | 6% |
| 2001 | | |
| 2003 | | |
| 2005 | 2,902 | |

Projected, based on 10%/increase per year

# Geriatric Population
## 60 and Older

| Year | Value | % Change |
|------|-------|----------|
| 1989 | | |
| 1990 | | 10% |
| 1991 | | 14% |
| 1992 | | 7% |
| 1993 | | 8% |
| 1994 | | 14% |
| 1995 | | 17% |
| 1996 | | 16% |
| 1997 | | 7% |
| 1998 | | 10% |
| 1999 | | 5% |
| 2000 | 1,353 | |
| 2001 | | |
| 2002 | | |
| 2003 | | |
| 2004 | | |
| 2005 | | |

August 7, 2000

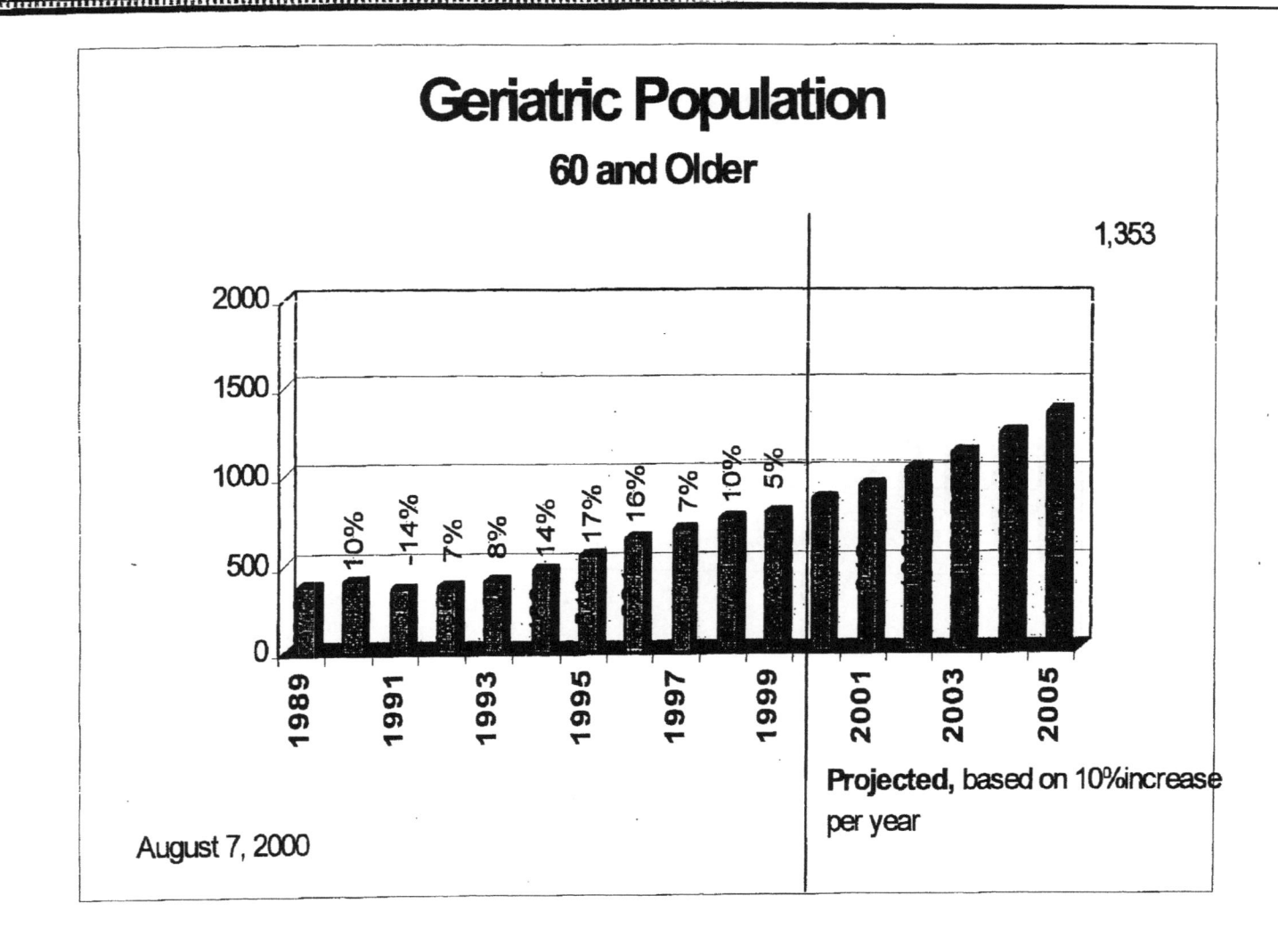

Projected, based on 10%/increase per year

# Important Facts About Elderly Inmates

◆ Due to their medical and social histories, i.e. drug use, high risk sexual behavior, smoking and neglect of health, inmates' appraised medical age is 5 to 10 years older than their chronological age.

◆ The cost of incarcerating a geriatric prisoner is about *three times* that of other prisoners and the most expensive portion of cost is for health care.

- Elderly inmates have special needs with respect to housing, work, social interaction, education (preparation for end of life), health care, self care, post-release placement and family interaction; however, most correctional systems are not yet fully prepared to address these needs.

- Prison systems are usually better established to deal with a younger population - in terms of education, housing, work programs, exercise, facility physical layout, food selections, etc.
- Correctional staff in many states have limited training pertaining to the management of elderly inmates.

- There is no consistent definition of "geriatric" or "elderly". Correctional systems typically designate the elderly population at age 50, 55 or 60. NIC recommends age 50 due to the poor health level of many older inmates.

- Some elderly inmates (aged 55+) suffer from 2-3 chronic conditions while incarcerated. Common health conditions include hypertension, cardiac, diabetes, skeletal/locomotor, and cognitive/intellectual problems.

# Why the Increase of Elderly and LTC in Prisons?

- Enactment of Tougher Sentencing Laws:
- "Three strikes"
- Federal truth-in-sentencing - 85% of sentence served
- Longer sentences
- Higher minimum amount of time until parole eligibility
- "Life Means Life Served"

# Improved Health Care

- New medical advances which elongate life to include significant advances in medications.
- Improved prison health care

# Parole Board Reduced Parole Approvals

- Sex offenders
- Violent offenders

# Limited Post-Release Placement for the Elderly and LTC

# Correctional Care Management Issues

◆ What kinds of support activities/services are needed and are appropriate to be provided?

◆ What managerial issues are raised?

◆ What are the implications for post-release planning and coordination with parole?

- Should efforts be made to provide alternative placement or should the elderly and LTC serve their sentences in prison?

- What is the impact to prison work assignments, counseling, classification, education and recreational activities?

- These questions are only a few of those which must be addressed as the elderly and LTC populations increase.

# Our Objectives For The Management And Care Of The Elderly And LTC Populations

- **Address all Aspects of Needs –**
  - Establish health care services adequate to meet the needs of our elderly and LTC populations.

- *Ensure Appropriate Accommodations –*
  - Designate LTC (skilled and personal) in facilities which provide the most suitable accommodations and environment by facilitating patient mobility and service delivery.

### Enhance Care and Interactions
- Establish in-service training for facility staff interacting with elderly and LTC inmates.

### Wise use of Staff Resources
- Improve nursing skills caring for both the elderly and LTC inmates. Include the use of certified nursing assistants. Use inmates in a non-medical support role.

## Number of Inmates Needing Assistance

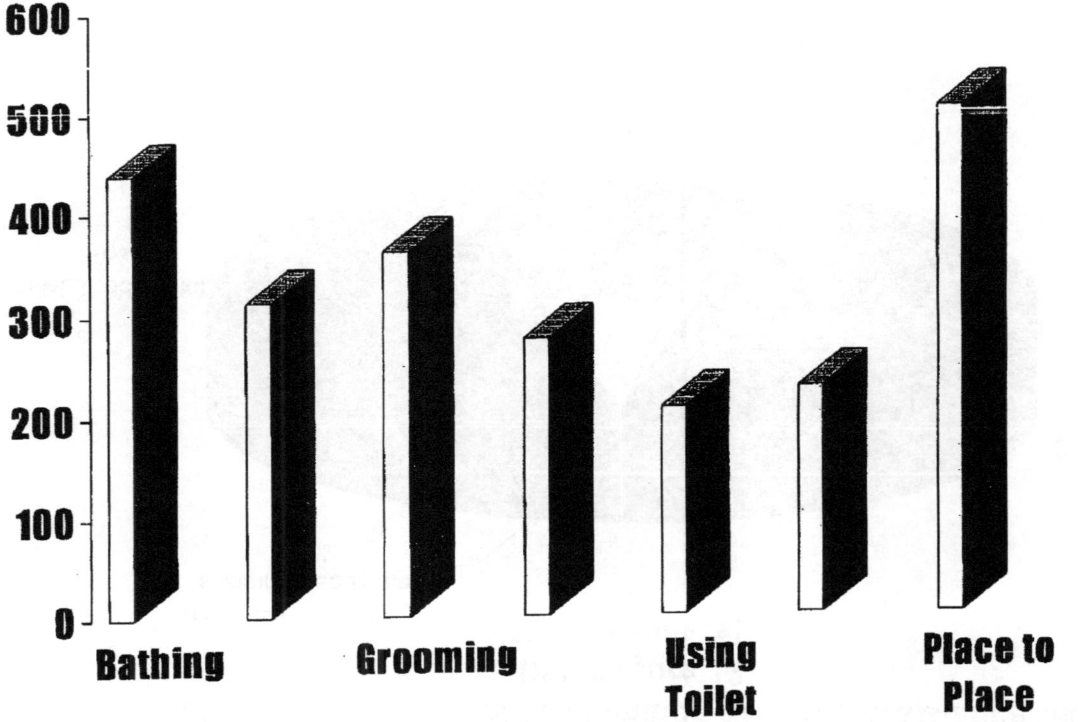

| Category | Approximate Number |
|---|---|
| Bathing | ~475 |
| Grooming | ~300 |
| Using Toilet | ~200 |
| Place to Place | ~550 |

## Primary Impairments of 624 Inmates Needing Assistance with ADL's (Figure 12)
[598 responses]

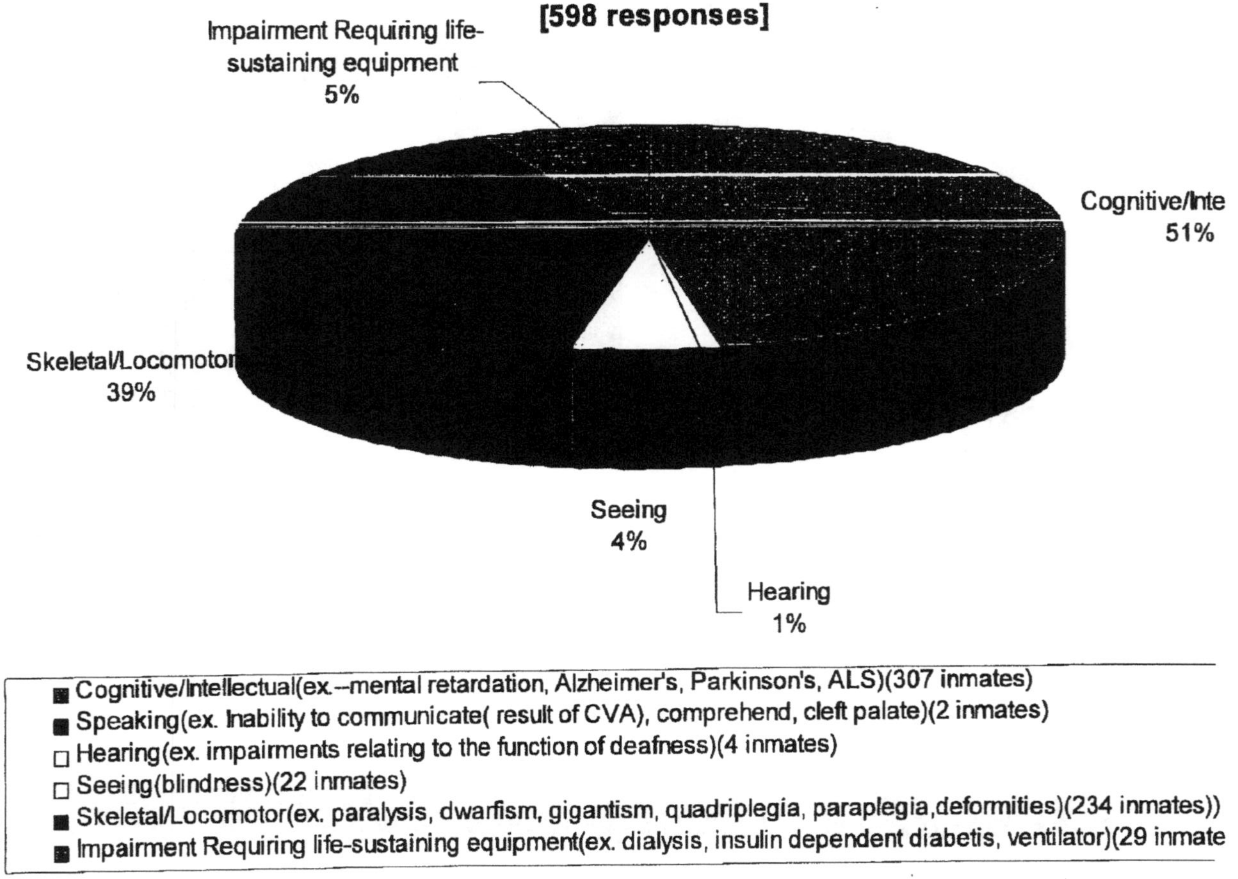

- Cognitive/Inte 51%
- Skeletal/Locomotor 39%
- Impairment Requiring life-sustaining equipment 5%
- Seeing 4%
- Hearing 1%

- Cognitive/Intellectual(ex.--mental retardation, Alzheimer's, Parkinson's, ALS)(307 inmates)
- Speaking(ex. hability to communicate( result of CVA), comprehend, cleft palate)(2 inmates)
- Hearing(ex. impairments relating to the function of deafness)(4 inmates)
- Seeing(blindness)(22 inmates)
- Skeletal/Locomotor(ex. paralysis, dwarfism, gigantism, quadriplegia, paraplegia,deformities)(234 inmates))
- Impairment Requiring life-sustaining equipment(ex. dialysis, insulin dependent diabetis, ventilator)(29 inmate

# Definitions

- **_Long term care refers to both personal care (also known as assisted living) and skilled care:_**

- **_Personal Care -_**

  The inmate maintains his independence and performs tasks with minimal assistance. The inmate can no longer function in the general population of the prison environment. The inmate typically requires verbal ques and prompting.

- **_Skilled Care -_**

  The inmate is routinely supervised by licensed personnel to provide individual nursing care, related medical, and other health services in a 24 hour period. The inmate is unable to care for himself.

# GERIATRIC PATIENTS
# IMPLICATIONS FOR THE CLINICIAN

- Mental illness plays an important role in 25 percent of suicides, and this percentage rises with age: from 50 percent in suicides who are over fifty years old to over 70 percent in suicides older than sixty.

- Most suicide attempts reflect a person's ambivalence about dying; patients requesting assisted suicide show an equal ambivalence. When interviewed two weeks after a request for assisted suicide, two-thirds of these patients show a significant decrease in the strength of the desire to die.

- Like other suicidal individuals, patients who desire an early death during a serious or terminal illness are usually suffering from a treatable depressive condition. Although pain and other factor, such as a lack of family support, contribute to their wish for death, depression is the most important factor, and researchers have found it to be the only factor that significantly correlates with the wish for death.

- Suicidal patients are especially prone to setting absolute conditions on life, such as: "I won't live...without my husband, " "if I lose my looks, power, prestige, or health," or "if I am going to die soon." These patients are afflicted by the need to make demands on life that cannot be fulfilled. Determining the time, place, and circumstances of their death is the most dramatic expression of their need for control.

- Patients who attempt suicide and those who request assisted suicide often test the affection and care of others. Expression such as, "I don't want to be a burden to my family," or " My family would be better off without me," usually reflect depressed feelings of worthlessness or guilt or may be a plea for reassurance. Not surprisingly, they are also classic indicators of suicidal depression in people who are in good physical health. Whether physically healthy or terminally ill, these individuals need assurance that they are still wanted; they also need treatment for their depression.

(geriatricpatients.6.8.01)

# Suicide Risk Profile Types
## Suicide Profile Type 1:
### Anxious/Agitated

- Depressed, with signs of agitation, ruminative anxiety, possible panic attacks, and insomnia-anxiety
- Often driven by delusional belief
- Often concealed by patient or "normalized" by patient or care staff
- Often no prior attempts; patient may deny suicidal thoughts or intent; agitation/anxiety is evidence of severe psychic pain

# Suicide Profile Type 2: Recurrent, Ruminative Anxiety

- Presentation with moderate depression, recurrent anxiety, sometimes panic attacks
  - Often ruminative anxiety, which as "obsessional" quality
  - Covert delusions may be present, even in high functional patients
- Patient may continue role function with periods of improvement punctuated by anxiety-depression recurrences
- Usually no prior history of suicide attempts or ideation

# Suicide Profile Type 3: Impulsive, With Substance Abuse

- Usually male, often sociopathic features
- Depression appears situational
- History of impulsive behavior and substance abuse; often, prior suicide threats or attempts
- Suicidal behaviors have "bargaining" quality
- Suicide usually occurs within 6 months of interpersonal loss, after "bargaining" fails; associated with substance use

# Suicide Profile Type 4: Impulsive, Angry, Anxious

◆ Often young, female, with borderline features
◆ History of suicide threats, attempts, angry dyscontrol
◆ Increasing anxiety, possible dissociative episodes, emotional lability, anger
◆ Suicide often takes place in context of actual or anticipated discharge or separation
◆ Attempts sometimes appear intended to elicit rescue, but are lethal

# General Data About Elderly Inmates

## NIC: Prison Health Care: Suicide Prevention

### Holistic Approach to Prison Suicide Prevention
### FRED R. MAUE, M.D.
### 6/26/01  10:15 – 12:00

OVERVIEW

Holistic Approach Schematic (Attachment 1)

Self-Injurious Behavior (SIB) vs. Parasuicidal Behavior (Attachments 2 & 3)

MAD vs. BAD – The Dilemma of "The Manipulative Inmate" (Handouts – 2 pages)

Scoring System For Serious Suicide Attempts (Attachment 4)

Rational Authority – Teamwork Approach To Good Decision-making (Attachment 5)

SAD Persons – No Hope – Risk Factor Profile (Attachment 6)

Holistic Approach.6.6.01

# HOLISTIC APPROACH TO SUICIDE PREVENTION IN PRISONS

**OPERATIONS**
Prison Housing
Staff Observation
Documentation Activity Logs
Screening (Referral) – Risk Factors
Intervention Measures
Response/Reporting (Tracking)
Extraordinary Occurrence Review

**INTERDISCIPLINARY**
Cross Training
Communication
Multidisciplinary Teams

Policies

Peer/Staff Awareness
Mortality Reviews

Critical Incident Stress Management
Aftercare Prevention
Rational Authority
Central Office Empowerment

**CLINICAL**
Assessment
Risk Factor Profile
Documentation in Medical Records
Clinical Intervention:
Crisis Intervention
Treatment:
Interpersonal Psychotherapy
Cognitive Behavioral
Medication
Aftercare Planning
Programs
Lifers
Spirituality
Anger management
Trauma Recover
Parenting
Restorative Justice
Vocational
Educational
Cultural Competency
Drug & Alcohol Prevention

Suicide Prevention.6.6.01

## SELF-INJURIOUS BEHAVIOR (SIB)

Any intentional act that results in organ or tissue damage to an individual, regardless of motivation or "mental state". This includes self-mutilation.

Often a building of intense, acute dysphoria that cannot be resolved non-destructively – the SIB is non-painful and dysphoria resolving.

## PARASUICIDAL BEHAVIOR

An apparent attempt at suicide, as by self-poisoning or self-mutilation, in which death is not desired outcome.

Self-Injurious Behavior.6.6.01

## SUICIDE INTENT

|  | YES | NO |
|---|---|---|
| Death | Completed | ? |
| Serious Injury | Serious Attempt | Parasuicide |
| No Serious Injury | Serious Attempt | Parasuicide |

Suicide Intent.6.6.01

# COMMONWEALTH OF PENNSYLVANIA
# STATE CORRECTIONAL FACILITY AT

_____

ject: **Evaluation of Inmate Self-Injury**   Date: _____

**Facility Manager**   RE: _____

Date of Injury: _____

om: **Deputy Superintendent**

CTORS INDICATING NEED/NO NEED FOR CLINICAL REVIEW ACCORDING TO 13.1.2

| ES | | NO | COMMENTS |
|---|---|---|---|
| ____ | 1. Suicide Death | ____ | _____ |
| ____ | 2. Attempt: | | |
| ____ |    Intent evident | ____ | _____ |
| ____ |    Method – lethal | ____ | _____ |
| ____ |    Conceal – reveal | ____ | _____ |
| |    Timing | ____ | _____ |
| ____ |    Motive | ____ | _____ |
| ____ | 3. Serious Harm Done | ____ | _____ |
| | 4. History: | | |
| ____ |    MH problems | ____ | _____ |
| ____ |    Prior attempts | ____ | _____ |
| ____ | 5. Foreseen/Preventable | ____ | _____ |
| | 6. Security actions | | |
| ____ |    Security | ____ | _____ |
| ____ |    Medical | ____ | _____ |
| ____ |    Mental Health | ____ | _____ |

_____ Recommendation _____
_____ Approval _____

**Proceed with clinical review**     **No clinical review required. Copy involved**
**In accordance with 13.1.2**     **Dept. Heads, Medical Record-Mental Health**
                                                 **Section, and Training Coordinator.**

DC-516

ional Authority means:

  (1) Firm structuring of treatment
  (2) Setting limits and controls
  (3) Establishing a graduated series of sanctions

itional Authority Implies:

  (1) A direct confrontation to the offender of:

      The realities and legitimate requirement of society in the prison setting

  (2) A full acceptance of the offender as a patient yet:

      Rejecting his unacceptable behavior

- YOU ARE ILL
- YOUR ILLNESS may not be under your control
- YOU may not be Responsible for your Behavior

YET: Your actions are not tolerable
     They must be controlled:

              By the offender (patient)
              By those charged with his/her care
                      (corrections)
                      (treatment)

## NIC: Prison Health Care: Suicide Prevention

### Holistic Approach to Prison Suicide Prevention
### FRED R. MAUE, M.D.
### 6/26/01  10:15 – 12:00

OVERVIEW

Holistic Approach Schematic (Attachment 1)

Self-Injurious Behavior (SIB) vs. Parasuicidal Behavior (Attachments 2 & 3)

MAD vs. BAD – The Dilemma of "The Manipulative Inmate" (Handouts – 2 pages)

Scoring System For Serious Suicide Attempts (Attachment 4)

Rational Authority – Teamwork Approach To Good Decision-making (Attachment 5)

SAD Persons – No Hope – Risk Factor Profile (Attachment 6)

Holistic Approach.6.6.01

# General Data About Elderly Inmates

# Suicide Profile Type 4: Impulsive, Angry, Anxious

- Often young, female, with borderline features
- History of suicide threats, attempts, angry dyscontrol
- Increasing anxiety, possible dissociative episodes, emotional lability, anger
- Suicide often takes place in context of actual or anticipated discharge or separation
- Attempts sometimes appear intended to elicit rescue, but are lethal

## Suicide Profile Type 3: Impulsive, With Substance Abuse

- Usually male, often sociopathic features
- Depression appears situational
- History of impulsive behavior and substance abuse; often, prior suicide threats or attempts
- Suicidal behaviors have "bargaining" quality
- Suicide usually occurs within 6 months of interpersonal loss, after "bargaining" fails; associated with substance use

# Suicide Profile Type 2: Recurrent, Ruminative Anxiety

- Presentation with moderate depression, recurrent anxiety, sometimes panic attacks
  - Often ruminative anxiety, which as "obsessional" quality
  - Covert delusions may be present, even in high functional patients
- Patient may continue role function with periods of improvement punctuated by anxiety-depression recurrences
- Usually no prior history of suicide attempts or ideation

# Suicide Risk Profile Types

## Suicide Profile Type 1: Anxious/Agitated

- Depressed, with signs of agitation, ruminative anxiety, possible panic attacks, and insomnia-anxiety
- Often driven by delusional belief
- Often concealed by patient or "normalized" by patient or care staff
- Often no prior attempts; patient may deny suicidal thoughts or intent; agitation/anxiety is evidence of severe psychic pain

# GERIATRIC PATIENTS
# IMPLICATIONS FOR THE CLINICIAN

- Mental illness plays an important role in 25 percent of suicides, and this percentage rises with age: from 50 percent in suicides who are over fifty years old to over 70 percent in suicides older than sixty.

- Most suicide attempts reflect a person's ambivalence about dying; patients requesting assisted suicide show an equal ambivalence. When interviewed two weeks after a request for assisted suicide, two-thirds of these patients show a significant decrease in the strength of the desire to die.

- Like other suicidal individuals, patients who desire an early death during a serious or terminal illness are usually suffering from a treatable depressive condition. Although pain and other factor, such as a lack of family support, contribute to their wish for death, depression is the most important factor, and researchers have found it to be the only factor that significantly correlates with the wish for death.

- Suicidal patients are especially prone to setting absolute conditions on life, such as: "I won't live...without my husband, " "if I lose my looks, power, prestige, or health," or "if I am going to die soon." These patients are afflicted by the need to make demands on life that cannot be fulfilled. Determining the time, place, and circumstances of their death is the most dramatic expression of their need for control.

- Patients who attempt suicide and those who request assisted suicide often test the affection and care of others. Expression such as, "I don't want to be a burden to my family," or " My family would be better off without me," usually reflect depressed feelings of worthlessness or guilt or may be a plea for reassurance. Not surprisingly, they are also classic indicators of suicidal depression in people who are in good physical health. Whether physically healthy or terminally ill, these individuals need assurance that they are still wanted; they also need treatment for their depression.

(geriatricpatients.6.8.01)

## Definitions

◆ **Long term care refers to both personal care (also known as assisted living) and skilled care:**

◆ **Personal Care -**

The inmate maintains his independence and performs tasks with minimal assistance. The inmate can no longer function in the general population of the prison environment. The inmate typically requires verbal ques and prompting.

◆ **Skilled Care -**

The inmate is routinely supervised by licensed personnel to provide individual nursing care, related medical, and other health services in a 24 hour period. The inmate is unable to care for himself.

## Primary Impairments of 624 Inmates Needing Assistance with ADL's (Figure 12)
[598 responses]

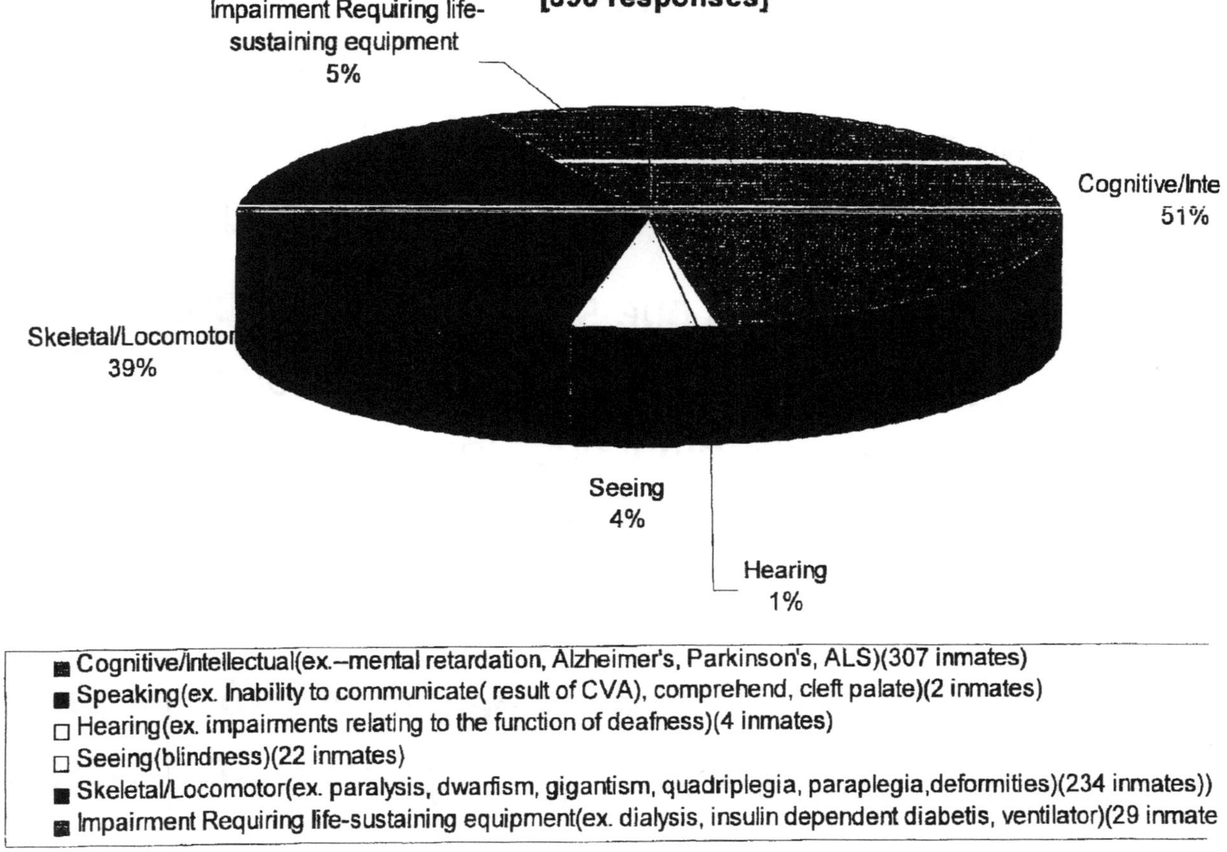

- Cognitive/Intellectual 51%
- Skeletal/Locomotor 39%
- Impairment Requiring life-sustaining equipment 5%
- Seeing 4%
- Hearing 1%

- Cognitive/Intellectual(ex.--mental retardation, Alzheimer's, Parkinson's, ALS)(307 inmates)
- Speaking(ex. Inability to communicate(result of CVA), comprehend, cleft palate)(2 inmates)
- Hearing(ex. impairments relating to the function of deafness)(4 inmates)
- Seeing(blindness)(22 inmates)
- Skeletal/Locomotor(ex. paralysis, dwarfism, gigantism, quadriplegia, paraplegia, deformities)(234 inmates))
- Impairment Requiring life-sustaining equipment(ex. dialysis, insulin dependent diabetis, ventilator)(29 inmate

## Number of Inmates Needing Assistance

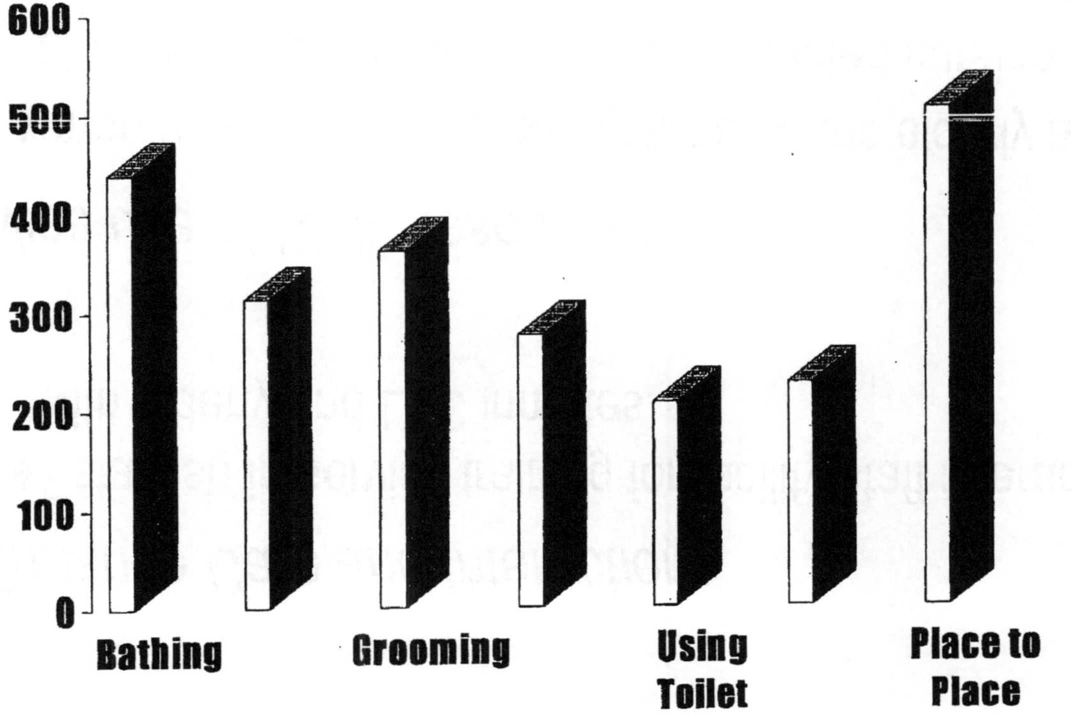

| Activity | Approximate Number |
|---|---|
| Bathing | ~475 |
| Grooming | ~275 |
| Using Toilet | ~150 |
| Place to Place | ~550 |

### ♦ *Enhance Care and Interactions*
- ♦ Establish in-service training for facility staff interacting with elderly and LTC inmates.

### *Wise use of Staff Resources*
- ♦ Improve nursing skills caring for both the elderly and LTC inmates. Include the use of certified nursing assistants. Use inmates in a non-medical support role.

# Our Objectives For The Management And Care Of The Elderly And LTC Populations

- **Address all Aspects of Needs** –
- **Establish** health care services adequate to meet the needs of our elderly and LTC populations.

- *Ensure Appropriate Accommodations* –
- **Designate** LTC (skilled and personal) in facilities which provide the most suitable accommodations and environment by facilitating patient mobility and service delivery.

- Should efforts be made to provide alternative placement or should the elderly and LTC serve their sentences in prison?

- What is the impact to prison work assignments, counseling, classification, education and recreational activities?

- These questions are only a few of those which must be addressed as the elderly and LTC populations increase.

# Correctional Care Management Issues

- What kinds of support activities/services are needed and are appropriate to be provided?

- What managerial issues are raised?

- What are the implications for post-release planning and coordination with parole?

- *Improved Health Care*
  - New medical advances which elongate life to include significant advances in medications.
  - Improved prison health care
- *Parole Board Reduced Parole Approvals*
  - Sex offenders
  - Violent offenders
- *Limited Post-Release Placement for the Elderly and LTC*

## Why the Increase of Elderly and LTC in Prisons?

- Enactment of Tougher Sentencing Laws:
- "Three strikes"
- Federal truth-in-sentencing - 85% of sentence served
- Longer sentences
- Higher minimum amount of time until parole eligibility
- "Life Means Life Served"

- There is no consistent definition of "geriatric" or "elderly". Correctional systems typically designate the elderly population at age 50, 55 or 60. NIC recommends age 50 due to the poor health level of many older inmates.

- Some elderly inmates (aged 55+) suffer from 2-3 chronic conditions while incarcerated. Common health conditions include hypertension, cardiac, diabetes, skeletal/locomotor, and cognitive/intellectual problems.

- Prison systems are usually better established to deal with a younger population - in terms of education, housing, work programs, exercise, facility physical layout, food selections, etc.
- Correctional staff in many states have limited training pertaining to the management of elderly inmates.

- Elderly inmates have special needs with respect to housing, work, social interaction, education (preparation for end of life), health care, self care, post-release placement and family interaction; however, most correctional systems are not yet fully prepared to address these needs.

# Important Facts About Elderly Inmates

- Due to their medical and social histories, i.e. drug use, high risk sexual behavior, smoking and neglect of health, inmates' appraised medical age is 5 to 10 years older than their chronological age.

- The cost of incarcerating a geriatric prisoner is about *three times* that of other prisoners and the most expensive portion of cost is for health care.

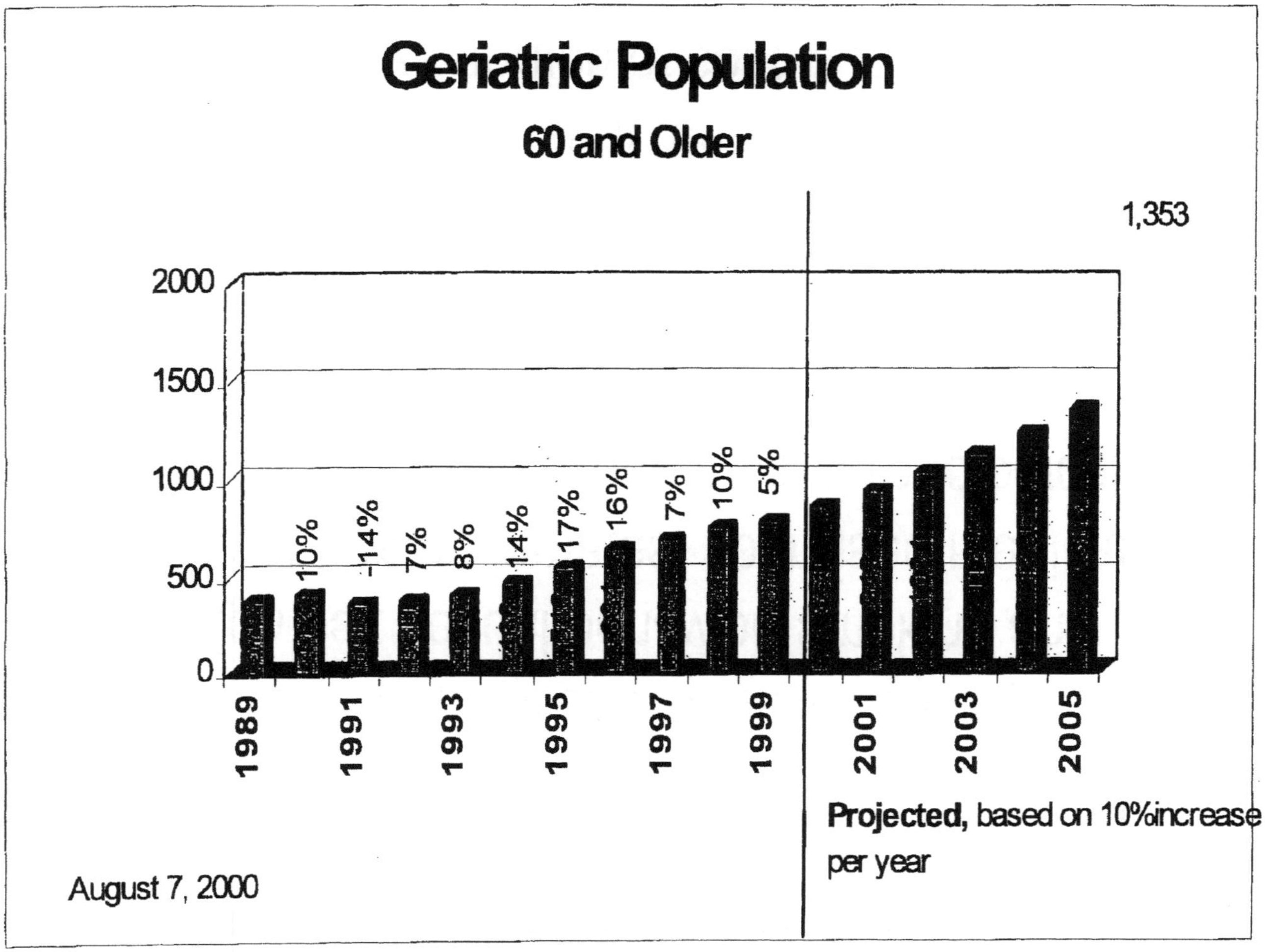

# Geriatric Population
## 60 and Older

| Year | Value | % Change |
|---|---|---|
| 1989 | | |
| 1990 | | 10% |
| 1991 | | 14% |
| 1992 | | 7% |
| 1993 | | 8% |
| 1994 | | 14% |
| 1995 | | 17% |
| 1996 | | 16% |
| 1997 | | 7% |
| 1998 | | 10% |
| 1999 | | 5% |
| 2000 | 1,353 | |
| 2001 | | |
| 2002 | | |
| 2003 | | |
| 2004 | | |
| 2005 | | |

Projected, based on 10%/increase per year

August 7, 2000

# Geriatric Population
## 55 and Older

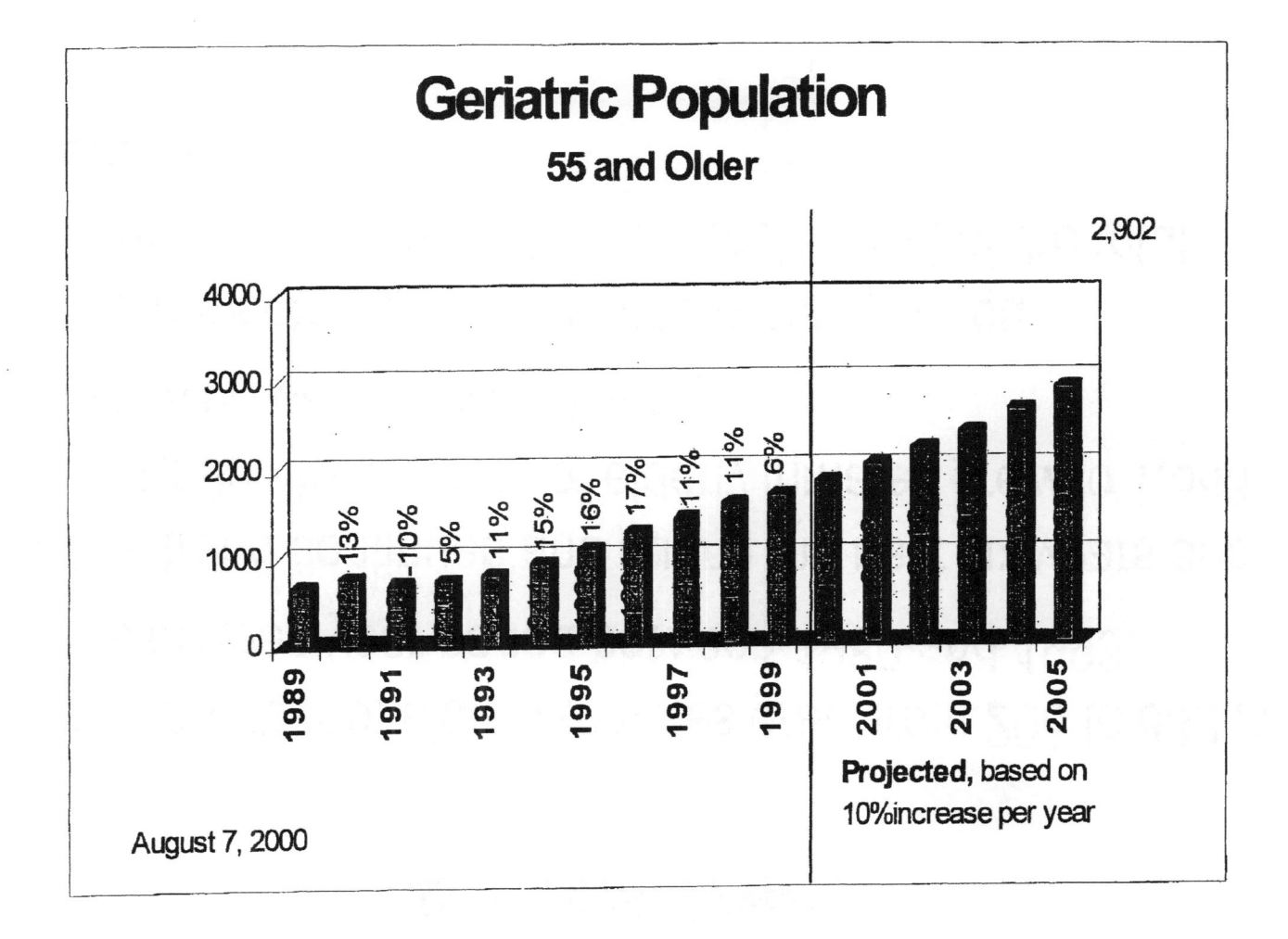

August 7, 2000

| Year | Change |
|------|--------|
| 1989 | |
| 1990 | 13% |
| 1991 | 10% |
| 1992 | 5% |
| 1993 | 11% |
| 1994 | 15% |
| 1995 | 16% |
| 1996 | 17% |
| 1997 | 11% |
| 1998 | 11% |
| 1999 | 6% |

Projected, based on 10% increase per year

2005: 2,902

## In Pennsylvania...

- The number of elderly inmates grew from 206 to 832 in the thirteen year period between 1980 and 1993.

- The trend continued and during the next six years and by 12/99, the number of elderly inmates grew to 1,683 (an average of 10% per year).

- It is projected that by the end of this year our population 55 and older will reach 1,832 of the total population.

## Trends in Aging...

◆ Individuals age 65 and older are the fastest growing age group in America.

◆ Correctional systems are also experiencing the aging of their inmate populations. The number of inmates 55 and older doubled in the 9 year period from 1981 to 1990. This inmate aging trend continued in the 1990's.

◆ From 1985 to 1997 1/3 of the state correctional systems experienced over a 400% increase in their age 50+ inmate populations.

# NIC PRISON SUICIDE PREVENTION TRAINING

Special Needs Offenders – Geriatric Inmates

Fred R. Maue, M.D.

# Superando El Momento

# Prevención de Suicidios en Las Cárceles

The Pennsylvania Department of Corrections gratefully acknowledges the contribution of NYS Office of Mental Health, Bureau of Forensic Services, Central New York Psychiatric Center

---

como tú, para muchas personas estos sentimientos surgen del hecho de estar encarcelados, por la muerte de algún familiar la ruptura de una relación íntima o por un sinnúmero de otras razones.

Es importante y difícil buscar ayuda en estos momentos. Cuando te sientes sin aliento no necesitas oír un sermón o consejo que te desanime mas. Necesitas a alguien que te escuche con el respeto que tu te mereces.

¡Nosotros tenemos una persona con quien puedes hablar y que puede ayudarte a manejar tus momentos de crisis!

La siguiente es como conseguir ayuda: Habla con su consejero o director de unitario. Puede ponerse en contacto con el departamento de psicológra como ponerse en el papel de cita. Es importante ponerse la sequiente información:

NOMBRE: _____ DOC Numero: _____
ELDA Numerro: _____ FECHA: _____

¡Es importante que sientas que tienes a alguien que te puede dar esperanzas!

## Como Reconocer Una Crisis

Las personas que han experimentado una crisis pueden haber intentado resolver sus problemas de todas las formas que han creído posible. Pero nada parece funcionar. Ellos pueden empezar a sentirse desesperanzados e inadaptados. Esto los asusta. De hecho, algunas personas peuden hacer lo imposible para escapar de esto.

Desafortunadamente, muchas personas sienten que ellos tienen que resolver sus problemas solos, sin ayuda. Creyendo que nada de lo que han tratado vale la pena, pueden hacerse daño. Esto puede deberse a que se encuentran tan metidos en sus

---

## Indicios de Suicidio

Las personas encuentran muchas maneras de decirles a otras cuanto sufren. Estas son algunas de las cosas que usted podría escuchar:

- No aguanto más.
- Ya nada importa.
- ¡Total, si no valgo nada!
- Mis familiares estarían mejor sin mi.

Estas son algunas de las conductas que manifiestan personas, que por sentirse tan mal, desean suicidarse:

- no cuidar de su apariencia o su salud.
- sentirse siempre cansado.
- no poder dormir en las noches.
- alejarse de los compañeros mas cercanos.
- sentirse nervioso o inquieto sin motivo.
- hablar sobre temas de muerte.
- hacerse cortes o quemaduras en el cuerpo o tratar de ahorcarse.
- guardar pastillas o medicamentos con la intención de tomarlas.
- repartir o regalar objetos personales de mucho valor sentimental.

Las personas que se comportan en esta forma, generalmente experimentan problemas emocionales y pueden estar considerando el suicidio.

## Que Puedes Hacer Por Los Demás

1. Mantener la calma.
2. Mostrar interés y preocupación por lo que pasa.
3. Escucharlo con respeto.
4. No darle consejos que puedan hacerlo sntir peor.
5. Avisarle al oficial de guardia que un compañero necesita ver un consejero para que le ayude.

# Living Through It

## Suicide Prevention

## For People in Prison

The Pennsylvania Department of Corrections gratefully acknowledges the contribution of NYS Office of Mental Health, Bureau of Forensic Services, Central New York Psychiatric Center

---

much hope for change? For many people, perhaps like yourself, these feelings may be due to incarceration, loss of a family member, the break-up of a close relationship, or one of any number of other reasons.

Reaching out is very important at times like this and is often very difficult. When you feel low, you don't need a lecture or advice that feels like a put down. You need someone who can listen to you with respect.

*We offer you someone to talk to, someone to help you cope with your crisis!*

Here is how to get that helping hand: Contact your Unit Counselor or Unit Manager. You may also contact the psychology department by submitting a request slip. Make sure you print the following information on the slip:

NAME:          DOC #:
CELL #:         DATE:

*Feeling like you have someone to talk with gives hope!*

## How To Recognize a Crisis

People who experience a crisis may have already tried everything they can think of to solve their problem. Nothing seems to work. They may begin to feel hopeless and inadequate. This can be really scary. In fact, some people may do almost anything to escape it.

Unfortunately, many people feel that they have to solve their problems alone. Not seeing anything worthwhile from what they have

---

problem to see their choices. This is why a trusted associate or a trained mental health counselor can be helpful.

## Clues To Suicide

People find many ways of telling others how much they hurt. These are some of the things you may hear:

- I can't take it any more.
- It won't matter soon.
- I'm no good anyway.
- My family would be better off without me.

These are some of the behaviors of people who hurt so much that they may want to attempt suicide:

- Neglect of appearance or health.
- Always tired.
- Drawing away from close associates.
- Sudden edginess or restlessness.
- Talk of death or dying.
- Cutting or burning oneself.
- Collecting pills or other medications.
- Giving away prized possessions.

People who are doing any combination of these things may be experiencing emotional problems. They may be thinking of suicide.

## What You Can Do For Others:

1. Stay calm
2. Show concern.
3. Listen with respect.
4. Don't give advice that sounds like a put down.
5. Tell the CO that an inmate needs to see a counselor for help.

**SUICIDE RISK INDICATORS CHECKLIST FOR RHU/SMU**      Revised (6/21/99)

TE NAME: _____  DOC #: _____
SMU Officer Completing Form (print): _____  Date: _____ Time: _____

| | | |
|---|---|---|
| l | 1. | Escorting officer has information that inmate may be a suicidal risk. |
| l | 2. | Inmate is expressing suicidal thoughts/making threats to harm self. |
| J | 3. | Inmate shows signs of depression (crying, withdrawn, passive). |
| J | 4. | Inmate is acting/talking in a strange manner (hearing/seeing things that aren't there). |
| √ | 5. | Inmate appears to be under the influence of drugs/alcohol. |
| √ | 6. | Inmate has recent family change (e.g., death of child/spouse/parent or "Dear John letter" |
| √ | 7. | Inmate has recent legal status change (e.g., parole violation or new detainer). |
| N | 8. | <u>Inmate states this is his/her first placement in RHU/SMU.</u> |
| N | 9. | Inmate has been assaulted (physically or sexually) by another inmate. |
| N | 10. | Inmate shows anger, hostility, and threats. |
| N | 11. | Inmate appears anxious, afraid (pacing, wringing hands). |
| N | 12. | Inmate displays signs of self-neglect or abuse (e.g., poor hygiene or cuts and bruises). |
| N | 13. | Inmate states that he/she is taking psychiatric medication. |

nments: _____

ructions: The ranking CO present shall ensure that this form is completed when an inmate is brought to the RHU/SMU. T orting officer will be asked (a) why the inmate is being brought in and (b) whether there is any information that the inmate m elf-destructive. The inmate will be asked (a) if this is his/her first time in the RHU/SMU, (b) if he/she has any speci lems or needs of which staff should be aware, (c) if he/she is on any medication, and (d) whether he/she has any rece l status changes (e.g., parole violation or detainer). The officer will also note any special physical/behavioral characteristi ., crying, poor hygiene, & cuts and bruises) or if the inmate is uncooperative.

y of items #1 through #8 are checked "Yes," the RHU/SMU officer shall immediately phone the following staff:

Between 8:00 AM and 4:30 PM, nursing and Chief Psychologist or MHC. Psychologist will immediately visit the RHU/SMU review the checklist, assess the inmate, and discuss the case with RHU/SMU staff. Time of assessment will be recorded form.

After hours, or on weekends, the nursing staff and Shift Commander. Nurse will immediately visit RHU/SMU to revie checklist, assess the inmate, and discuss case with RHU/SMU staff. Time of assessment will be recorded on form.

At any time the inmate appears in immediate danger of harming him/herself or somebody else, the RHU/SMU staff sh also contact the Shift Commander, as well as nursing staff and Chief Psychologist or MHC to request an immedia assessment.

y of items #9 through #13 are checked, the form will be submitted to the nurse and/or psychologist the next time they visit U/SMU, but within 24 hours. The nurse or psychologist will assess the inmate and note the date and time of assessment. T npleted form will remain in the Cumulative Adjustment Record until reviewed by PRC. Copies to Medical Record & DC-

nical Staff Action: _____
_____ Date: _____ Time: _____
me of Clinical Staff (printed): _____ Title: _____

## Selected Bibliography

Cheek, F. E. (1983, February). Correctional Officer Stress. *Corrections Today*, 14, 15, 18 24.

Cooperstein, M. A. (2001, May). Corrections Officers: The forgotten police force. *Pennsylvania Psychologist Quarterly*, 61(5), 7, 18, 19, 23.

Couturier, L.C. and Maue, F.R (2000, summer). Suicide prevention initiatives in a large, statewide Department of Corrections. Jail Suicide/Mental Health Update, 9 (4), 1-8.

Jamison, K. R. (1999). *Night falls fast: Understanding suicide.* New York: Alfred A. Knopf.

4. Mandate anti-suicide smocks and blankets

C. Expand continuum of mental health treatment services for inmates with mental illness – present mental health services brochure

D. Divert inmates with mental illness from placement in administrative segregation, whenever possible.

E. Disseminate suicide prevention and mental health information to inmate population.

1. Publish suicide prevention brochure, printed in English and Spanish – present brochure.

2. Produce suicide prevention videotapes, in English and Spanish, to be presented to all inmates via institution's closed circuit television networks. —Show sample film from SCI-Coal or Smithfield

F. Increase comprehensiveness of clinical reviews (psychological autopsies) following all suicides and frequency of review following serious attempts.

G. Enhance programming and services for non-mentally ill inmates, including sex offenders, substance abusers, elderly inmates, and "lifers" and long term offenders

VII. Mechanisms to provide emotional support to PA Department of Corrections staff members

A. Critical Incident Stress Management (CISM)
B. Suicide prevention training.
D. Development of benefits brochure highlighting CISM, SEAP (State Employees Compensation), and Workmen's compensation.

B. Abusers of alcohol and other drugs (AOD) – however, most inmates display AOD problems.

C. Male inmates – PA DOC has only had 2 female suicides since 1992; however, women compose on 4% of the DOC population.

D. White inmates – Caucasians compose 34% of the population, but account for 54 to 89% of the suicides.

E. Elderly inmates

F. Sex offenders

G. Lifers and long term offenders

H. Parole violators

I. Inmates in Community Corrections Centers (CCC's).

J. Surprisingly, we have not encountered suicides in the youthful offenders.

V. Staff suicide is a serious problem in the PA Department of Corrections

A. Staff members are also at risk of stress related problems – correctional staff members die earlier and display higher incidents of divorce, alcoholism, stroke, hypertension, heart attaches, and suicides than civilians in the community.

B. Suicide is a significant risk factor among Corrections Officers, being 39% higher compared to the working age population.

C. In 2000, there were 3 staff suicides in a work force of approximately 14,000.

VI. PA Department of Corrections initiatives to reduce suicides

A. Comprehensive initial and on going and "cross-training" are cornerstones of suicide prevention.

B. Rewrite suicide prevention policies and develop other formal mechanisms to force better communication and collaboration between custody and clinical staff members.

1. Write-in extensive cross-references in custody and treatment policies

2. Employ "Suicide Risk Indicators Checklist for RHU's/SMU's"

3. Mandate use of 911 Emergency tools

NIC PRESENTATION
LANCE COUTURIER, PH.D.

## SUICIDE PREVENTION IN THE DEPARTMENT OF CORRECTIONS
May 30, 2001

I. Introductory Exercise: How many know someone (family or friend) who killed self)? What were your reactions? [Audience responses recorded on flip chart.]

II. Pennsylvania Department of Corrections suicide statistics:

| | Year | Suicides | | Population |
|---|---|---|---|---|
| A. | 1989 | 8 | (3rd in nation) | 18 - 19,000 |
| B. | 1990 | 7 | | 19 - 20,000 |
| C. | 1991 | 3 | | 23,000+ |
| D. | 1992 | 4 | | 24,000+ |
| E. | 1993 | 2 | | 25,000+ |
| F. | 1994 | 6 | | 26,000+ |
| G. | 1995 | 14 | | 30,000+ |
| H. | 1996 | 10/11* | | 34,000+ |
| I. | 1997 | 8/9* | | 35,000+ |
| J. | 1998 | 11 | | 36,000+ |
| K. | 1999 | 8/9* | | 36,000+ |
| L. | 2000 | 5 | | 36,000+ |
| M. | 2001 | 2** | | 36,000+ |

*In 1996, 1997, and 1999, there were suicides in the Community Corrections Centers (CCC's)

**A fatal drug overdose is under investigation

III. Means of suicide in PA prisons [Present overhead]

A. Hanging – almost all PA DOC suicides have been hangings, with a few overdoses – stress all that is needed is pressure on the carotid artery, and brain damage occurs in 4 minutes and death in 6 minutes.

B. Cutting – until 1998 in PA DOC we had seen no fatal cuttings – there were 2 in 1998, both were inmates with heinous homicide offenses.

C. Over-dosing on drugs and/or alcohol

D. Bizarre self-mutilations by inmates with mental illness

IV. Inmate suicide risk factors in the PA Department of Corrections. Many are similar to risk factors in the community.

A. Inmates with mental illness – 14% of population, but 69% of suicides

# HOLISTIC APPROACH TO SUICIDE PREVENTION IN PRISONS

| OPERATIONS | INTERDISCIPLINARY | CLINICAL |
|---|---|---|
| Prison Housing | Cross Training | Assessment |
| Staff Observation | Communication | Risk Factor Profile |
| Documentation Activity Logs | Multidisciplinary Teams | Documentation in Medical Records |
| Screening (Referral) – Risk Factors | Policies | Clinical Intervention: Crisis Intervention |
| Intervention Measures | Peer/Staff Awareness | Treatment: |
| Response/Reporting (Tracking) | Mortality Reviews | Interpersonal Psychotherapy |
| Extraordinary Occurrence Review | Critical Incident Stress Management | Cognitive Behavioral |
| | Aftercare Prevention | Medication |
| | Rational Authority | Aftercare Planning |
| | Central Office Empowerment | Programs |
| | | Lifers |
| | | Spirituality |
| | | Anger management |
| | | Trauma Recover |
| | | Parenting |
| | | Restorative Justice |
| | | Vocational |
| | | Educational |
| | | Cultural Competency |
| | | Drug & Alcohol Prevention |

## SELF-INJURIOUS BEHAVIOR (SIB)

Any intentional act that results in organ or tissue damage to an individual, regardless of motivation or "mental state". This includes self-mutilation.

Often a building of intense, acute dysphoria that cannot be resolved non-destructively – the SIB is non-paintful and dysphoria resolving.

## PARASUICIDAL BEHAVIOR

An apparent attempt at suicide, as by self-poisoning or self-mutilation, in which death is not desired outcome.

Self-Injurious Behavior.6.6.01

## SUICIDE INTENT

|  | YES | NO |
|---|---|---|
| Death | Completed | ? |
| Serious Injury | Serious Attempt | Parasuicide |
| No Serious Injury | Serious Attempt | Parasuicide |

Suicide Intent.6.6.01

## COMMONWEALTH OF PENNSYLVANIA
## STATE CORRECTIONAL FACILITY AT

Subject: **Evaluation of Inmate Self-Injury**     Date: _____

         **Facility Manager**     RE: _____

         Date of Injury: _____

From: **Deputy Superintendent**

FACTORS INDICATING NEED/NO NEED FOR CLINICAL REVIEW ACCORDING TO 13.1.2

| YES | | NO | COMMENTS |
|---|---|---|---|
| ____ | 1. Suicide Death | ____ | _____ |
| ____ | 2. Attempt: Intent evident | ____ | _____ |
| ____ |     Method – lethal | ____ | _____ |
| ____ |     Conceal – reveal | ____ | _____ |
| ____ |     Timing | ____ | _____ |
| ____ |     Motive | ____ | _____ |
| ____ | 3. Serious Harm Done | ____ | _____ |
| ____ | 4. History: MH problems | ____ | _____ |
| ____ |     Prior attempts | ____ | _____ |
| ____ | 5. Foreseen/Preventable | ____ | _____ |
| ____ | 6. Security actions — Security | ____ | _____ |
| ____ |     Medical | ____ | _____ |
| ____ |     Mental Health | ____ | _____ |

_____ Recommendation _____
_____ Approval _____

**Proceed with clinical review In accordance with 13.1.2**      **No clinical review required. Copy involved Dept. Heads, Medical Record-Mental Health Section, and Training Coordinator.**

DC-516

ional Authority means:

(1) Firm structuring of treatment
(2) Setting limits and controls
(3) Establishing a graduated series of sanctions

tional Authority Implies:

(1) A direct confrontation to the offender of:

The realities and legitimate requirement of society in the prison setting

(2) A full acceptance of the offender as a patient yet:

Rejecting his unacceptable behavior

YOU ARE ILL
YOUR ILLNESS may not be under your control
YOU may not be Responsible for your Behavior

YET: Your actions are not tolerable
They must be controlled:

By the offender (patient)
By those charged with his/her care
(corrections)
(treatment)

## SAD PERSONS  NO HOPE

Sex--men commit suicide 3x more than women
Age--Elderly at highest risk  prison 31-40
Depression--or hopelessness

Previous attempt
Etoh abuse (consider drug abuse also)
Rational thinking loss (psychosis)
   also consider Relative-has a relative committed suicide--
   family history
Social supports-lack of
Organized plan
No spouse
Sickness (medical) and mental illness (esp thought
   disorder.  10% of Schizophrenic pts commit suicide

---

No frame work for meaning
Overt change in clinical condition

Hostile interpersonal environment (RHU)
Out of hospital recently
Predisposing personality factors
Excuses for dying are present and strongly believed

---

# JAIL AND PRISON SUICIDE LITIGATION: CASE LAW REVIEW

*Listed below are case summaries of significant jail and prison suicide litigation compiled by Lindsay M. Hayes. This listing is not intended to be all inclusive. Revised May 2001.*

1) *Tittle v. Jefferson County Commission* [10 F. 3rd 1535 (11th Cir. 1994)]. Between October 1987 and December 1989, 57 suicide attempts occurred in the county jail, including four successful suicides within the 12-month period of September 1988 and 1989. The majority of these incidents involved hangings from various window bars or pipes in the facility. Each pipe, measuring six inches in diameter and filled with concrete, was located approximately four feet above the bed and bolted to concrete blocks in front of the window in each cell. In its first opinion [(966 F.2d 606 (11th Cir. 1992)], the appeals court stated that "*it is true that prison officials are not required to build a suicide-proof cell. By the same token, however, they cannot equip each cell with a noose.* It falls to the plaintiff on remand to establish that defendants were deliberately indifferent to the probability that inmates would attempt to commit suicide by hanging themselves from the bar."

In the second opinion, after an *en banc* review of the first decision, the court overturned the verdict by stating that the prior history of suicides did not show that "all prisoners of the Jefferson County Jail are substantially likely to attempt suicide." In the midst of this prolonged litigation, the defendants covered up the pipes in question, as well as updated its intake screening and staff training policies.

2) *Natriello v. Flynn* [837 F. Supp. 17 (D. Mass. 1993) and 36 ATLA L. Rep. 368 (Dec. 1993)]. In *Natriello*, the 19-year-old decedent was incarcerated in a county jail in January 1989. During the intake assessment, he reported a prior history of IV drug use, a suicide attempt, family history of both suicidal behavior and substance abuse, and the recent death of his grandfather. The decedent was also suffering from hepatitis. During seven months of incarceration, he engaged in aggressive, combative and self-destructive behavior resulting in both disciplinary confinement and observation under suicide watch. On August 18, 1989, the decedent engaged in self-destructive behavior, was transported to the local hospital for treatment of injuries, and subsequently returned to the jail and again placed under suicide watch. Less than two days, he was found hanging from a ceiling grate in his cell by a bed sheet. The medical examiner later determined that the decedent had been dead for approximately five to seven hours prior to being found.

During the jury trial, the plaintiff offered evidence that the two officers assigned to the unit housing the decedent on suicide watch were either laying down and/or sleeping in the control booth with the lights out for the majority of their shift. In addition, the officers were not supervising the activities of an "inmate watcher," who was assigned to sit in a folding chair in the corridor and monitor the decedent as well as a second suicidal inmate in an adjacent cell during an eight-hour shift. The inmate watcher allegedly left his post unattended after three hours. In addition, evidence was offered to suggest that suicide prevention policies and staff training were grossly inadequate, and that cells designated to house suicidal inmates were dangerous. The jury returned a verdict in favor of the plaintiff. In lieu of appeal, both sides subsequently agreed to a negotiated settlement of approximately $230,000.

3) *Heflin v. Stewart County* [958 F.2d 709 (6th Cir. 1992)]. A deputy went to the decedent's cell on September 3, 1987 and saw a sheet tied to the cell bars. The deputy immediately went to the dispatcher's office, told the dispatcher to call the sheriff and ambulance service, picked up the cell block keys, and returned to open the cell. When the deputy entered the cell, he observed the decedent "hanging by the neck on the far side of the shower stall." The decedent's hands and feet were tied together, a rag was stuffed in his mouth, and his feet were touching the floor. With the body still hanging, the deputy checked for a pulse

and signs of respiration, but found none though the body was still warm. He also opened the decedent's eyes and found the pupils were dilated. From these observations the deputy concluded that the decedent was dead. While the deputy was still alone in the cell with the hanging body, a jail trusty arrived with a knife he had picked up in the kitchen. Rather than utilize the knife to cut the decedent down, the deputy ordered the trusty out of the area. The sheriff arrived shortly thereafter and directed the deputy to take pictures of the decedent before he was taken down.

At trial, the plaintiffs introduced evidence that the defendant maintained a policy of leaving victims as discovered, despite the medical procedures available to resuscitate victims. They ultimately prevailed and a jury awarded damages to the decedent's family based upon proof that the defendants' acted with deliberate indifference after discovering the decedent hanging. The defendants appealed by arguing that the decedent was already dead and their action or inaction could not have been the proximate cause of his death. The appeals court ruled that "there clearly was evidence from which the jury could find that Heflin died as the proximate result of the failure of Sheriff Hicks and Deputy Crutcher to take steps to save his life. They left Heflin hanging for 20 minutes or more after discovering him even though the body was warm and his feet were touching the floor...The unlawfulness of doing nothing to attempt to save Heflin's life would have been apparent to a reasonable official in Crutcher or Hick's position in 'light of pre-existing law'..." The court also affirmed the award of damages in the amount of $154,000 as well as approximately $133,999.50 in attorney fees.

See also *Tlamka v. Serrell* [8th Circuit, No. 00-1648, March 2001], in which the court ruled that three correctional officers could be sued for allegedly ordering inmates to stop giving CPR to an inmate who collapsed in a prison yard following a heart attack. The court stated that "any reasonable officer would have known that delaying Tlamka's emergency medical treatment for 10 minutes, with no good or apparent explanation for the delay, would have risen to an Eighth Amendment violation."

4) *Simmons v. City of Philadelphia* [947 F.2d 1042 (3rd Cir. 1991)]. The decedent was arrested for public intoxication and transported to a police precinct lockup for "protective custody." He was initially described by the arresting officer as being heavily intoxicated, agitated, and crying. During the first few hours of incarceration, the booking officer periodically observed the decedent as having "glassy eyes...in a stupor" with behavior ranging from confusion to hysteria. The booking officer subsequently discovered the decedent hanging from the cell bars by his trousers. He was cut down and paramedics were called, but the booking officer did not initiate any life-saving measures. The plaintiff filed suit alleging that the city violated the decedent's constitutional right to due process "through a policy or custom of inattention amounting to deliberate indifference to the serious medical needs of intoxicated and potentially suicidal detainees." At trial, the plaintiff offered evidence which showed that from 1980 through 1985, the city's police department experienced 20 suicides in its lockups, did not provide suicide prevention training to its officers nor intake screening for suicide risk to its inmates, or any other suicide prevention measures.

In affirming the jury verdict, the appeals court stated that "the evidence of 20 jail suicides in the Philadelphia prison system between 1980-85, of whom 15 were intoxicated, *the City's possession of knowledge before 1981 that intoxicated detainees presented a high risk of suicide, its awareness of published standards for suicide prevention, and its failure to implement recommendations of experts, including its own director of mental health services for the prison system, was sufficient basis for the jury to have found the unnamed officials with responsibility over the City's prisons acted recklessly or with deliberate indifference, thereby contributing to the deprivation of constitutional rights of plaintiff's decedent If a city cannot be held liable when its policy makers had notice of a problem and failed to act, then it is difficult to posit a set of facts on which a city could be held liable to have been deliberately*

that he and Deputy Rabalais made periodic checks on Jacobs; however, it is unclear exactly how often the deputies checked on Jacobs while she was under the "precautionary" suicide watch. What is clear is that as many as 45 minutes elapsed from the time a deputy last checked on Jacobs to the time she was discovered hanging from the light fixture in the detox cell.

Specifically, the record reveals that, after having observed Jacobs in the detox cell at 12:22 a.m. and 1:00 a.m., Deputy Reech checked on Jacobs at 1:22 a.m., and he observed her lying awake in her bunk. At 2:00 a.m., Deputy Rabalais went to investigate some loud music down the hall, and on his way back to the control station, he observed Jacobs lying awake in her bunk. Deputy Rabalais testified that both he and Deputy Reech checked on Jacobs sometime between 2:00 and 2:44 a.m., and that Jacobs was still awake in her bunk. After this last check, Deputy Reech returned to the jail lobby to read his newspaper. At approximately 2:44 a.m., Deputy Rabalais looked into the detox cell from the control room and saw what appeared to be part of an arm hanging from the ceiling. Concerned, he went to find Deputy Reech, who was still reading the newspaper, to help him get into the detox cell. When the deputies arrived at the cell, they found Jacobs hanging from a sheet that had been tied around the caging surrounding a ceiling light fixture. Deputy Rabalais found a knife and enlisted the assistance of another inmate in cutting the sheet and lowering Jacobs onto the floor. By all indications, Jacobs had torn a small string from the bunk mattress and wrapped that string around the sheet to form a make-shift rope. The paramedics who arrived only moments later were unable to resuscitate Jacobs. Jacobs's suicide was the third suicide at the jail during Sheriff Daniel's tenure there. As noted above, James Halley's suicide had occurred in the same cell where Jacobs killed herself. The third suicide had occurred in a cell down the hallway from the detox cell. The family of Sheila Jacobs filed suit.

On September 13, 2000, the United States Court of Appeals for the 5th Circuit ruled that the family had sufficient grounds to sue then-Sheriff Bill Daniel and Deputy Rabalais. The court stated, in part, that:

"The record before us reveals that Sheriff Daniel was aware that Jacobs had tried to kill herself once before and that she posed a serious risk of trying to do so again. Throughout the time Jacobs was in the jail, Sheriff Daniel considered her to be a suicide risk. Under Sheriff Daniel's supervision, Jacobs was placed in the detox cell, which had a significant blind spot and tie-off points, despite the fact that during Sheriff Daniel's tenure another detainee, James Halley, had committed suicide in the same cell by hanging himself from one of the tie-off points....Moreover, Sheriff Daniel ordered his deputies to give Jacobs a blanket and towel, despite the fact that he still knew that she was a suicide risk. He did not offer any reason for doing so other than Jacobs's appointed counsel's suggestion that she be given these items, and in fact, he acknowledged that a suicidal person should not have loose bedding of any kind in a cell with them. Sheriff Daniel also acknowledged that it was not advisable to place a suicidal detainee in a cell with tie-off points, even though the detox cell had tie-off points. We note also that with full awareness that a prior suicide occurred in the detox cell by way of an inmate securing a blanket to a tie-off point therein, Sheriff Daniel did nothing to eliminate or conceal the tie off points in the detox cell, which cell Sheriff Daniel's own unwritten policy mandated as the appropriate cell for housing suicidal detainees....*We would find it difficult to say that this behavior could not support a jury finding that Sheriff Daniels acted with deliberate indifference, and likewise we find it even more difficult to say that this conduct was objectively reasonable.* For these reasons, as well as for substantially the same as those reasons given in the Magistrate Judge's order denying summary judgment, we affirm the denial of qualified immunity for Sheriff Daniel as to claims asserted against him in his individual capacity....

....Deputy Reech was the senior deputy on duty when Jacobs killed herself. Like Sheriff Daniel and Deputy Rabalais, he had actual knowledge that Jacobs was a suicide risk at all times during her detention. He also knew about the earlier hanging suicide of James Halley in the detox room, and with respect to the Halley and Jacobs suicides, Reech deposed that there was nothing they (at the jail) could do to stop the detainees from killing themselves if they wanted to and that it wasn't their responsibility. Despite this knowledge, and the fact that nothing had been done to correct either the blind spot or the tie-off points in the detox cell, Deputy Reech ordered Jacobs to be placed in it for a suicide watch. Like Sheriff Daniel, Deputy Reech was on notice that these facilities were 'obviously inadequate'....

....We note that it was Sheriff Daniel, not Deputy Reech, who made the decision that Jacobs be given a blanket. The fact that Reech did not make the decision that Jacobs should have a blanket would seem to militate in favor of finding qualified immunity, since after all, if no blanket had ever been provided, it would not have made any difference which cell he had placed her in. On the other hand, Deputy Reech did observe Jacobs lying on the bunk in the detox cell several times during the period when she had the sheet, and despite his awareness that a prior suicide occurred in the detox cell using a blanket and that suicidal inmates should not be given lose bedding, he did not take the sheet away from Jacobs. Additionally, Deputy Reech did not check on Jacobs as frequently as he was supposed to....

....Given Deputy Reech's level of knowledge about the significant risk that Jacobs would attempt to harm herself and his disregard for precautions he knew should be taken, we conclude that there is enough evidence in this record from which a reasonable jury could find subjective deliberate indifference. And in light of Deputy Reech's failure to insure that adequate precautions were taken to protect Jacobs from her known suicidal tendencies, we find that Deputy Reech's conduct falls outside the realm of that which could be characterized as being objectively reasonable in light of the duty to not act with subjective deliberate indifference to a known substantial risk of suicide....

....We conclude that no reasonable jury could find that Deputy Rabalais, who had only been on the job for about six months at the time of Jacob's death, acted with deliberate indifference, and we further find that his conduct, in light of the record evidence, was objectively reasonable, thus entitling him to qualified immunity from suit in his individual capacity. While Deputy Rabalais, like his co-defendants, had actual knowledge that Jacobs was a suicide risk at all times during her confinement, he did not make the decision to place her in the detox cell. As noted above, Deputy Reech, the senior deputy on duty with over twenty years of experience, made that decision. Deputy Rabalais likewise had nothing to do with the order that Jacobs be given a blanket and towel, which order was evidently interpreted by some unknown jail official as entitling Jacobs to a loose sheet instead....

....The only element of Jacobs's detention over which Deputy Rabalais had direct control was the frequency with which he checked on her. Like Deputy Reech, Deputy Rabalais did not comply with Sheriff Daniel's unwritten policy of checking on Jacobs every fifteen minutes. However, this failure to abide by Sheriff Daniel's policy alone evinces at best, negligence on the part of Deputy Rabalais, which is insufficient to support a finding of deliberate indifference....

....As a result of the foregoing analysis, we dismiss this appeal as it relates to the official capacity claims asserted against Sheriff Daniel for a lack of interlocutory appellate jurisdiction, we affirm in part the Magistrate Judge's order to the extent that it denies summary judgment on grounds of qualified immunity on the individual capacity claims asserted against Sheriff Daniel and Deputy Reech, and we reverse in part the Magistrate Judge's order to the extent it denies summary judgment on grounds of qualified immunity on the individual capacity claims asserted against Deputy Rabalais and we remand to the district court for entry of judgment in his favor."

# MORTALITY REVIEW OF INMATE SUICIDES AND THE CASE OF GEORGE MOFFAT[1]

Presented by
**LINDSAY M. HAYES**
for
National Institute of Corrections
Prison Health Care: Suicide Prevention Workshop (01-P603)
Longmont, Colorado
June 2001

### THE CASE

On the evening of May 17, 1997, George Moffat (a pseudonym) was arrested for domestic violence against his wife Sheila and transported to a county jail in a midwestern state. During transport, he tried to cut his wrists while handcuffed in the back of the patrol car. Although the wounds appeared superficial, Mr. Moffat was transported to the local hospital for medical treatment. "It's a common thing. People cut their wrists thinking it will keep them out of jail. It doesn't work," commented Matthew Stevens, the arresting and transporting officer.

Upon arrival at the county jail, Mr. Moffat was booked and processed without incident, although jail staff determined that he was currently on probation for burglary. Nurse Laura Thompson completed a medical intake screening form. The 54-year-old inmate listed several problems, including gout, high blood pressure and back pain. Mr. Moffat also admitted that he had attempted suicide approximately four months ago by cutting his wrists, and had spent three days in the state hospital. No mention was made of the wrist cutting in the patrol car a few hours earlier and Mr. Moffat denied any current suicidal ideation. Although Nurse Thompson did not feel that his prior suicide attempt several months earlier justified any current preventative measures, as a precautionary matter, she filled out a referral slip for further assessment the following morning by the facility's mental health staff. The referral slip was placed in the mental health services' mailbox in the receiving and discharge unit. Mr. Moffat was then classified and subsequently placed in a general population housing unit.

George Moffat remained in the county jail for approximately six months. During this time, he received medical treatment when requested for his gout, high blood pressure, and back pain. He never requested mental health services, nor was he ever assessed by clinicians as a result of Nurse Thompson's initial referral. Mr. Moffat appeared in court several times, eventually pleading guilty to the domestic violence charge and receiving a county jail sentence. A separate hearing on whether to revoke his probation, which in all likelihood would result in a state prison sentence, was scheduled for the first week of December 1997. During his six months of incarceration, Mr. Moffat had little contact with his family. His two adult daughters refused to visit him in jail and his wife had contacted an attorney with the intent of filing for divorce.

---

[1] In order to ensure complete confidentiality, the names of the victim, facility, and staff have been changed. No other modifications to the facts of this case have been made.

On Saturday, November 22, 1997, Mr. Moffat called his wife over a dozen times and threatened to kill himself if she filed for divorce. He also appeared distraught at the prospect of going to prison. During one telephone call, Mr. Moffat told his wife that he was tearing his bed sheet into strips. Because she had heard her husband threaten suicide in the past and, in fact, he had attempted suicide at the same facility the previous year, Sheila Moffat was concerned about her husband's state of mind and called the county jail. She spoke with Lieutenant Skip Morrow who gave assurances that her husband would be safe. Following the telephone conversation, Lieutenant Morrow went to Mr. Moffat's housing unit and instructed Officer Daniel Anders to check the inmate's cell. When Officer Anders approached the cell he noticed that a strip of bed sheet was tied to the cell bars. Mr. Moffat was sitting on his bunk and appeared nervous. When the officer inquired as to why the cloth was tied to the bars, Mr. Moffat offered no explanation other than to deny that he was contemplating suicide. Officer Anders removed the cloth from the bars, confiscated the remainder of the bed sheet, and reported back to Lieutenant Morrow. The officer was instructed to write a report of the incident (to include the fact that Mr. Moffat had denied being suicidal) and forward a copy to mental health staff.

During the next several hours, Officer Anders checked Mr. Moffat's cell on an hourly basis. The inmate appeared to be sleeping during a cell check at 11:10 pm. However, during a cell check at approximately 12:07 am on November 23, the officer observed George Moffat sitting on the floor with his back to the cell door. The leg of his jumpsuit was tied around his neck and through the cell bars. Officer Anders ran back to the control booth in the housing unit, instructed an officer to call for back-up support and medical personnel, grabbed a pair of medical shears from the first aid kit, and returned to the cell. The officer used the shears to cut the cloth away from the bars. Mr. Moffat's body fell to the floor. Other correctional staff arrived, the cell door was opened, and the inmate was pulled out into the hallway. An officer checked for vital signs and found none. Although trained in cardiopulmonary resuscitation (CPR), the officers did not initiate CPR, rather they waited for medical staff to arrive. A jail nurse arrived several minutes later and initiated CPR, assisted by a correctional officer who used a mouth shield from a pouch attached to his belt. Emergency Medical Services personnel arrived at 12:16 am and continued CPR. Mr. Moffat was subsequently transported to the hospital and pronounced dead upon arrival. Following his death, timely notification was made to both designated facility officials and Mr. Moffat's family.

Several investigations were conducted into the suicide of George Moffat. The first inquiry was the medical autopsy in which a forensic pathologist concluded that the cause of death was "asphyxia due to hanging." Next, the state police conducted an inquiry. A state trooper interviewed several correctional staff, reviewed incident reports from all involved staff, and inspected the cell area. His investigation lasted almost a full day and a subsequent two-page report concluded that the death was a suicide with no signs of foul play.

As per departmental policy, the county jail's mental health services administrator also reviewed Mr. Moffat's suicide. The inquiry was limited to a review of the inmate's medical file, and did not include any staff interviews. The mental health administrator summarized her document review of George Moffat's suicide in a one-paragraph confidential report self-titled a "psychological autopsy." The report is reprinted in its entirety as follows:

> The inmate, George Moffat, was admitted to the county jail on May 17, 1997. This inmate had written several medical requests, all of which were related to such discomforts as foot problems, colds, lower back pain, and rashes. He never requested mental health assistance, therefore Mental Health Services never had an opportunity to interview, evaluate or treat him throughout the six months of his incarceration. Based upon a review of the medical file, there is no evidence that this inmate's death could have been prevented.

The mental health administrator, however, did conduct a one-hour suicide prevention workshop for correctional staff several months after Mr. Moffat's death, the first such training for any departmental personnel in over 10 years.

George Moffat's suicide was also reviewed by the county prosecutor's office. An investigator from that office reviewed both Mr. Moffat's institutional and medical file, state police report, autopsy report, and transcription of the coroner's inquest. Based upon this review, the county prosecutor wrote a letter to the county sheriff which stated, in part, that "we limited the scope of our investigation to reviewing whether or not George Moffat died as a result of an unlawful homicide or suicide. It is clear that he died from his own actions. It is impossible to determine whether or not this inmate intended to take his own life. He may well have died accidentally while feigning suicide. Quite frankly, that was not really our concern. He clearly died by his own actions. We consider this case closed."

Shortly after receiving the county prosecutor's letter, Sheriff Roy Hamilton issued a press release on April 27, 1998 stating that George Moffat's suicide had been investigated thoroughly by several agencies and each concluded that there was no criminal wrongdoing by any county jail personnel. When asked by a local newspaper reporter the following day whether he planned to make any changes in the 850-bed jail in light of Mr. Moffat's death, as well as two other inmate suicides during 1997, Sheriff Hamilton responded that "as far as we are concerned, this matter is over. There was no criminal involvement here. My concern is more if we suspect foul play. I have no idea why these inmates commit suicide in my jail. If I did, I could probably do a better job of preventing it."

## MORTALITY REVIEW OF AN INMATE SUICIDE

*The purpose of a mortality review of an inmate suicide is straightforward: What happened in the case under review and what can be learned to reduce the likelihood of future incidents. The mortality review team must be multidisciplinary and include correctional, mental health and medical personnel. Exclusion of one or more disciplines will severely jeopardize the integrity of the mortality review. Detailed below is a suggested format and areas of inquiry for conducting a mortality review.*

1) **Training**

   o Had all correctional, medical, and mental health staff involved in the incident previously received training in the area of suicide prevention?

   o Had all staff who responded to the incident previously received training (and are currently certified) in standard first aid and cardiopulmonary resuscitation (CPR)?

2) **Identification/Screening**

   o Had the inmate been properly screened for potentially suicidal behavior upon entry into the facility?

   o Did the screening include inquiry regarding: past suicidal ideation and/or attempts; current ideation, threat, plan; prior mental health treatment/hospitalization; recent significant loss (job, relationship, death of family member/close friend, etc.); history of suicidal behavior by family member/close friend; suicide risk during prior confinement; arresting/transporting officer(s) believes inmate is currently at risk?

   o If the screening process indicated a potential risk for suicide, was the inmate properly referred to mental health and/or medical personnel?

3) **Communication**

   o Was there information regarding the inmate's prior and/or current suicide risk from outside agencies that was not communicated to the correctional facility?

   o Was there information regarding the inmate's prior and/or current suicide risk from correctional, mental health and/or medical personnel that was not communicated throughout the facility to appropriate personnel?

   o Did the inmate engage in any type of behavior that might have been indicative of a potential risk of suicide? If so, was this observed behavior communicated throughout the facility to appropriate personnel?

4) **Housing**

   o Where was the inmate housed and why was he/she assigned to this housing unit?

   o Was there anything regarding the physical design of the inmate's cell and/or housing unit that contributed to the suicide (e.g., poor visibility, protrusions in cell conducive to hanging attempts, etc.)?

5) **Levels of Supervision**

   o What level and frequency of supervision was the inmate under immediate prior to the incident?

   o Given the inmate's observed behavior prior to the incident, was the level of supervision adequate?

   o When was the inmate last physically observed by staff prior to the incident?

   o If the inmate was not physically observed within the required time interval prior to the incident, what reason(s) was determined to cause the delay in supervision?

   o Was the inmate on a mental health caseload? If so, what was the frequency of contact between the inmate and mental health and personnel? When was the inmate last seen by mental health personnel?

   o If the inmate was not on a mental health caseload, should he/she have been?

   o If the inmate was not on suicide watch at the time of the incident, should he/she have been?

6) **Intervention**

   o Did the staff member(s) who discovered the inmate follow proper intervention procedures, i.e., surveyed the scene to ensure the emergency was genuine, called for back-up support, ensured that medical personnel were immediately notified, and began standard first aid and/or CPR?

   o Did the inmate's housing unit contain proper emergency equipment for correctional staff to effectively respond to a suicide attempt, i.e., first aid kit, pocket mask or mouth shield, Ambu bag, and rescue tool (to quickly cut through fibrous material)?

o Were there any delays in either correctional or medical personnel responding immediately to the incident? Were medical personnel properly notified as to the nature of the emergency and did they respond with appropriate equipment? Was all the medical equipment working properly?

7) **Reporting**

o Were all appropriate officials and personnel notified of the incident in a timely manner?

o Were other notifications, including the inmate's family and appropriate outside authorities, made in a timely manner?.

o Did all staff who came into contact with the inmate prior to the incident submit a report and/or statement as to their full knowledge of the inmate and incident? Was there any reason to question the accuracy and/or completeness of any report and/or statement?

8) **Follow-up**

o Were all affected staff and inmates offered critical incident stress debriefing following the incident?

o Were there any other investigations conducted (or that should be authorized) into the incident that may be helpful to the mortality review?

o Were there any findings and/or recommendations from previous mortality reviews of inmate suicides that were relevant to this mortality review?

o As a result of this morality review, what recommendations (if any) are necessary for revisions in policy, training, physical plant, medical or mental health services, and operational procedures to reduce the likelihood of future incidents.

Developed by Lindsay M. Hayes

Lightning Source UK Ltd.
Milton Keynes UK
UKHW050749261022
411121UK00009B/284